I0424086

TRUMP AND US POLITICS

Will His Empire Survive?

By Mohammed Helal

All rights reserved. Copyright @ 2016 Mohammed Helal

No part of this book may be reproduced, stored in a retrieval system, or transmitted in any form by any means without the prior permission of the publisher.
All opinions and beliefs expressed in this non-fiction work are solely that of the author. They do not represent the views of the publishing company.

ISBN-13: 978-1532939938
ISBN-10: 1532939930
US Library of Congress Control Number: 2016907391

CreateSpace Independent Publishing Platform
North Charleston, South Carolina
U.S.A.

Introduction

The Republican Party front-runner Donald Trump, a dazzling businessman of the American brand, with a New York flair, has his own way of creating and designing his business brand. He has been using his sheer power and talents through harsh industrial competitiveness and innovative dynamics.

In the US Presidential Election - 2016, he is in a political campaign and has already capitalized on right-wing Americans' anger with Washington's politicians, discomfort with immigration and fears of Muslim terrorism, attracting the lowest common denominators of the Republican electorates with his blatant talk and provocative postures, and the simply-worded promise to make America great again.

Donald Trump's ascension to the leadership of the right wing of American politics, and perhaps of the Republican Party, marks a milestone in American History. It is a stunning blow to many, but never was impossible. Donald Trump is leading a populist revolution in the USA. Media elites, political pundits, electoral analysts and the GOP establishment (GOP is the acronym for Grand Old Party, a nickname for the Republican Party) are struggling to understand what is happening with their predictions on Trump. Even if he burns out, some Americans, especially right-wing populists, find in him the characteristics of a greater leader to follow, and build their dreams and world around him.

Here we are focusing on Donald Trump, his followers, US cultures, and the world attitude toward this new phenomenon, and the reaction of the media. But it doesn't matter whether he wins or loses in this election year. Rather, what matters to some is to understand how this can happen in the establishment of the Republican Party. Will all the beaconing political ideologies be offset by this newborn culture of violent and incendiary remarks? Are we still short of calling it a newborn fascism, on the greatest hegemonic nation's own land?

The purpose of the book is soul-searching about Donald Trump and his followers, to understand their mindsets with different and historical references, to know his life, business, business branding, the attributes behind his success and the nature of his current political campaign. I have also tied up the destiny of his empire with or without the final win in this political campaign. Let's see how far we can go by digging in the soil of democratic America.

Who Is Donald Trump?

The host of the CBS late night show Stephen Colbert describes Trump: "He's like your dumb uncle who only knows what's on the internet." The right wing populists say, Trump is their savior, their renewed hope, while the left wing and the liberals say Trump is the worst demagogue of the 21st century. The drop-out Marco Rubio said, "He doesn't qualify to be our commander-in-chief."

"Who do you like better, President Obama or Donald Trump?" Jimmy Kimmel asked Ted Cruz in his Late Night Show. Ted replied, "I dislike Obama's policies more, but Donald is a unique individual," giving a look indicating that he absolutely can't stand Donald. Then he made it clear he would even run over the tycoon with a car if he had the chance!

"I will say, I was watching the early part of the show and if were in my car and getting ready to reverse, if I saw Donald in my back-up camera, I'm not confident which pedal I'd push," he revealed to loud applause. Hah! The Americans love that Ted got so real on the topic.

Let's see who is Donald Trump and how his business branding developed over the generations. Donald Trump's grandfather Friedrich Dumpf's ancestors settled in Germany's Kallstadt region in south-western Germany in the 1600s, carrying the soon-altered surname Drumpf. The family worked in their own vineyards.

Donald's great-grandfather was not interested in working in family vineyards but became a barber by profession, running his own business. He died at a young age. His son Fredrich Drumpf didn't follow his father's profession.

Fredrich was highly ambitious, wanted a life, a very dazzling life with more money, more fortunes than a barbershop could generate. This was impossible in Germany during that period of time. One day, he wrote a letter to his widowed mother and left it on the kitchen table. He started his lone journey to the West, to the USA, seeking his fortune. In 1885, Friedrich Drumpf stepped off a boat in lower Manhattan with a single suitcase. He was only sixteen years old, and his eyes were filled with glittering dreams of a fortune.

In New York, he lived in an immigrant apartment with his sister and brother-in-law for six years and worked, ironically, as a barber.

Within the first five years of his adventurous life, he had made some significant changes, which vastly improved his ability to compete in the growing labor market in the USA. He anglicized his first name from Fredrich to Frederick; grew from a skinny teenager into a big man with a moustache, and got US citizenship, which was an easy matter at a time when there were no immigration quotas and no waiting period for the application process. He had already learnt good English and US Entrepreneurship. After few years' living in New York, he moved to the West, to the young timber town of Seattle, a wide-open city, famous for its lumber industry boom. That was a big and bold move by this young man.

But migrant people in Seattle were soon disappointed because of the still incomplete recovery from the 1893 economic panic. However, Fredrick did not stop and waste his time. He worked in restaurants as a waiter, bouncer, and manager, earning enough cash to buy tables and chairs for a restaurant. He opened a restaurant in Seattle, but wanted more than conventional business practices would provide.

Fredrick became ambitious and moved to a prime location, the city's red-light district, widely known as the Lava Beds. He leased a tiny storefront restaurant named The Poodle Dog, which was always busy. This restaurant had a kitchen and a wet bar, and he advertised "private rooms for ladies" – a code for prostitutes in those days. It would allow the resourceful Fredrick, who renamed it the Dairy Restaurant, to offer the restless, disappointed, frustrated fortune-hunters in Seattle some instant satisfaction in the form of food, booze, and easily available sex. He was getting lot of cash.

But again, this cash flow was not enough for young and restless Fredrick. He was looking for a better opportunity. His next big move was influenced by a great advertisement, which was heralded on the front page of the newspaper *The Seattle Post-Intelligencer*, dated July 17, 1897. It had the big, bold headline: "Gold! Gold! Gold!" The picture was attractive to newcomers looking for fortunes and a better life. This Klondike gold rush actually started in 1896, but the news reached Seattle late.

This famous daily newspaper of the town excelled at sensationalizing stories, and attracting the interest of un-employed newcomers in Seattle.

It published a stunning, glittering picture of the port of Seattle showing huge amounts of gold and men returning from the "New Eldorado" with fortunes as high as $100,000, which was a fortune at that time. Gold in Klondike, Yukon, Canada, was discovered on August 17, 1896, had already become one of the world's largest gold rushes.

In a few days, the town of Seattle became busy with the throngs of prospectors, generally referred to as fortune-hunters. Soon, they started heading north to the Yukon, Canada, on a perilous journey by foot and snow sledges across snow-covered, rugged mountain passes.

Fredrick Trump was attracted by the newspaper stories and planned to leave for Yukon. Within months, he sold everything, including his two Seattle eateries, and also a piece of land in nearby Monte Cristo, Washington State.

Soon he joined a caravan of prospectors with his cash. He boarded a crowded ship to Alaska, hiked over mountains, passed through the Canadian Customs Agency, and to the mystic and mesmerizing Yukon River where he built a boat from scratch and transported a year's worth of personal supplies.

Through this big and risky move, Fredrick reached the golden goose, and found the golden eggs he had come to the United States for. However, it happened not in the United States but in Canada. This less publicized Canadian chapter in the life of Fredrick was important and then pivotal for him, his fortune and his descendants.

Then came in harsh Canadian winter, with bone chilling weather. In the journey to Yukon, he had to pass through notorious mountain passes, especially the White Pass. People were hungry, exhausted and dying, so were the animals. Owners whipped their tired and exhausted horses, donkeys, mules, oxen, carrying their personal things, and dogs pulling their sledges until they fell on the ground. These dead animals' bodies were neither buried nor even moved. The US National Parks Service estimates 3,000 animals died at the deadly White Pass during the gold rush, with many bones still visible today along so-called Dead Horse Trail.

The young and energetic German entrepreneur smelled opportunity. However, he had no intention of doing manual labor in the gold mines or the creeks, frenetically searching for gold. Instead he made a smart move; he and a similarly entrepreneurial friend named Ernest Levin set up a tent at this Dead Horse Trail. These two partners became friends soon and began to sell hot, simple meals to the constant stream of prospectors passing through. One of the bestselling items was made from the meat of frozen dead horses.

They made good money, and a few months later, these two brave and smart fortune-hunters moved their business from the lowly tent to a two-story building in Bennett Town, Northern BC, Canada. That was a big move in those days. They named it "The New Arctic Restaurant and

Hotel." This hotel soon became a paradise for newly wealthy single men. There were back room arrangements for the ladies. The hotel was located in the sea of tents surrounding it. In contrast, the town's restaurant was poor and dilapidated. Again, they planned to move to make more money, and at last, moved to Whitehorse, Yukon, close to the Klondike gold rush.

That was a very successful move. Hungry and rich were swarming their restaurant, which was located in a two-storey, wood-framed building. Their establishment gained a reputation as the finest eatery of its time in this booming area. They offered duck, caribou, salmon and oysters, and many varieties of berries. The business looked honest and prosperous, but actually this restaurant offered more than food.

Fredrick Drumpf was solely focused on making money, piling up his fortunes. The bulk of their cash came from the sale of liquor and sex. Their newspaper ads obliquely referred to prostitution—mentioning private suites for ladies, and scales in the rooms so patrons could weigh gold if they preferred to pay for services that way.

The provision of such female services was part of the regular restaurant package in those towns, and it isn't clear how the arrangement worked for both parties, but obviously, they were effective. Fredrick designed a unique business branding, new in that place, but a copy of what he had done in the red-light district of Seattle. Their business was going well and Fredrick was building his fortune, his dream coming true. The restaurants soon became boisterous with drunks, their booze and their women.

The Canadian Mounties (RCMP) initially allowed the rowdiness in these restaurants in the booming town. There were exceptions though, as described by Canadian writer Pierre Berton. "People faced forced labor or even banishment from this town if they cheated at cards; made a public ruckus; or partied on the Lord's Day."

If the RCMP's Major Wood, in charge of Klondike, actually had strictly enforced the laws in the red-light district regarding prostitution, gambling, and liquor, then hotels and restaurants would have been far less profitable and buzzing. Furthermore, the economic boom created by these newcomers with cash would have been short lived.

The RCMP Major understood that there was not nearly enough solid and sustainable economic development in that community to absorb these newcomers for any long-term period. WHEN the gold deposits were emptied, they would go back home. Without the umbrella of honey gold and its bees with liquid cash, other local industries would not be strong enough to keep going on their own in this cold North, and to compete with cheaper sources farther south. And he was right. This led to the establishment of Dawson City in 1896 and subsequently, the Yukon Territory in 1898. The Klondike gold rush solidified the public's image of the North as more than a barren wasteland and left a body of literature that has popularized and romanticized the Yukon Territory.

"Saloons and dance halls, theatres and business houses were shut tight one minute before midnight on Saturday," Berton wrote in his book "Klondike Fever."

One Yukon Sun writer wrote in a simplified way with a didactic, humble tone about the exciting backroom arrangements: "For single men, the 'Arctic' was the best restaurant, but I would not advise respectable women to go there to sleep as they are liable to hear that which would be repugnant to their feelings and uttered, too, by the depraved of their own sex."

But their good time didn't last that long. By early 1901, trouble began to threaten the rising community. The Royal Canadian Mounties (RCMP) announced their plans to eradicate prostitution, and curb gambling and liquor in this town. Fredrick quarreled with his partner and friend Ernest Levin. Gold finds were getting scarcer.

Frederick Trump realized that the gold boom was over, but he had already curved out a good fortune in a very unusual way in Yukon and kept it because of his frugality. Above all, he had achieved the craft of business branding for himself and for his grandson Donald Trump. In short, he had created a family culture of doing whatever it takes to come out on top and never giving up. While most of the miners were losers, he became a winner in a unique way.

Now he wanted to find a wife for himself. But he decided not to do it in America, rather in Germany, at his home, in his mother's presence. He returned to his homeland with US $582,000 in today's currency, and met a lady, Elizabeth. However, he was treated by the German Government as a draft-dodger in the German military for being away from his own country for a long time and becoming a U.S. citizen during his military draft years. Eventually, he faced tax fraud.

He married Elizabeth but soon, he was deported from Germany. He boarded a ship for New York with his wife, who was pregnant with Donald's dad, Fred Christ Trump. They Anglicized their last name from Drumpf to Trump. When they returned to New York, they settled down in a single-family house in Woodhaven, Queens. Donald's father Christ Trump was born in 1905, then they had two other children.

In New York, Donald's grandfather got involved in the real estate business. He opened a modest real estate agency in Queens, New York. He died of pneumonia in the 1918s influenza epidemic, leaving behind some real estate. He held mortgages for 16 Queens property owners, investments in stocks and bonds, a life insurance policy worth $450 and about $2,000 in cash. He had already paid $194 for his cemetery plot, $502 to his undertaker and $258 for a monument.

Soon after his father's death, 15-year-old Frederick Christ Trump went into the real estate and construction business with his mother Elizabeth. Their company, Elizabeth Trump & Son Co. was growing steadily.

During the 1920s and 30s, Fred Christ Trump focused on building affordable single-family houses in Brooklyn and Queens. He was a perfectionist in his construction business, who insisted on using quality materials regardless of the price of the home. He used to go to his work sites routinely and supervise his work crews closely.

In 1930, 18-year-old, beautiful Mary MacLeod, who was born in Tong, Scotland in 1912, sailed for America from Glasgow on the S.S. Transylvania, according to a copy of the ship's passenger list on Ancestry.com. MacLeod arrived in New York. She met Fred Christ Trump and they married in 1936. Donald's father was building the empire in New York and his business was staggering even through the Great Depression.

They had five children. Fred Christ Trump sometimes took the children with him on inspection tours of his properties. As always the frugal businessman, Trump used to save unused nails, mix his own floor cleaner, and personally handle the extermination work at some properties.

But he was not a clean businessman. Occasionally, he got involved in corruption and bribery scandals in New York.

Fred Christ Trump used to believe in the old school promotional strategy. Sometimes, their company, Elizabeth Trump & Son Co. released balloons at Coney Island containing coupons for $50 off the $4,990 purchase price of a Trump home. It worked well.

During WWII, Trump built housing developments for U.S. Navy personnel near the large East Coast shipyards, and made a huge profit off them. After the war, he built middle-income homes for returning veterans and their families. His Beach Haven development had 2,700 apartments. Trump Village had 3,800. Over the next decades, the company expanded into rental properties. He had made tens of millions and was living with five children in twenty-three rooms, nine bathrooms, a portico like Tara's suburban charm, in Jamaica Estates, Queens.

Donald John Trump was born in June 14, 1946 in this Estate of Queens, New York City, the fourth of five children of Frederick C. and Mary MacLeod Trump.

He was an energetic and bright, but very aggressive as well. He punched his music teacher because he didn't think he knew anything about music, and he almost got expelled from school, saved only because of his father's handsome donations. Later, Donald commented on this incident, "I'm not proud of that, but it's clear evidence that even early on I had a tendency to stand up and make my opinions known in a very forceful way. The difference now is that I use my brain instead of my fists."

Fred Christ Trump saw the wild streaks of adolescence in him, and sent him to the New York Military Academy at age thirteen, hoping the discipline of the school would channel his energy in a positive, emphatic manner. It worked perfectly for all. Trump did well at the academy, both socially and academically, rising to be a star athlete, to be the captain of the baseball team, a captain of a regiment and a student leader by the time he graduated in 1964. He was well-disciplined, and learnt leadership skills.

"They straightened him out," his father recalled. "He was a real leader," his baseball coach Colonel Theodore Dobias commented, "He was even a good enough first-baseman that the White Sox sent a scout to look at him."

During summers, Trump worked for his father's company at the construction sites in the boroughs and gained valuable experience under his father's careful guidance and mentoring. Soon, he entered Fordham University and then transferred to the famous Wharton School of Finance at the University of Pennsylvania, which was reputed to have one of the best schools on real estate in the US. He was doing well in his classes but developed a bit of cockiness. Some called it a youthful brashness, others arrogance, which was somewhat condescending as well. Now, in his campaign, we can see that this attitude has fully bloomed. From Wharton, he graduated in 1968 with a degree in Economics.

Later, Donald said he used these years in school to sort out his ideas and plans for his real estate business.

Immediately after graduation, Donald joined the company, bringing his plans and ideas in real estate. In 1968, Fred C. Trump had built over 27,000 low-income attached-apartments in Brooklyn and Queens, and was worth about $300 million.

Before graduating from the University of Pennsylvania, Donald had already worked with his father on developments in Queens and Brooklyn, gained valuable experience before purchasing or building multiple properties in New York and Atlantic City, New Jersey. Those properties included Trump Tower in New York, and Trump Plaza and multiple casinos in Atlantic City.

At his office, on Avenue Z, New York, Fred Christ Trump taught the business to his sons, showed how to crush opponents. Donald is the most successful one, because he designed a successful branding for his business.

Since the beginning of his career, Donald J. Trump has been continually setting standards of excellence while expanding his inexorable interests in real estate, sports, and entertainment through different financially challenged periods and thus become the typical definition of American business success story. He is the classic businessman of New York City – a real deal maker.

Trump began to work in his father's office in Sheepshead Bay, Brooklyn, New York and continued working with his father for five years, while his father was mentoring him and they were busy making business deals together. Donald Trump has been quoted as saying, "My father was my mentor, and I learned a tremendous amount about every aspect of the construction industry from him." Likewise, Fred Christ Trump often and proudly commented on his son, "Some of my best deals were made by my son, and Donald...everything he touches seems to turn to gold." He further said, "I gave Donald free rein." Donald Trump then entered the very different and difficult world of Manhattan real estate, surprisingly, continuing his success in business and creating a unique business branding. In New York City and around the world, the Trump signature began to be synonymous with the most prestigious of addresses and architecture.

In 1999, Fred Christ Trump died of pneumonia at a hospital in Queens, aged 93. He was one of the last of New York City's major post WWII builders and constructors. He was stricken with Alzheimer's disease six years previously, but still retained his title of Chairman of the Board of Trump Management, which he'd held since the company was formed in the mid-1960s. He was very frugal and did not believe in displays of flashes of wealth – with one exception. For decades, he had driven on one brand of Cadillac – always navy blue, always polished and shining, and always replaced every three years. His "FCT" license plate, heralding silently its proud owner wherever he went, was very familiar to the New Yorkers.

He was a punctual, polite and inquisitive man. According to his sons, he used to routinely drive his blue Cadillac to one of his many construction sites after his day's work. He was flamboyant. He used to wear an old, trimmed and neat suit while working. With his strong body-frame, chiseled features and wide grin, he resembled a silent-film star. But this businessman would pay meticulous attention to his business, his construction sites, walk through the studs and across the plywood floors of the homes under construction.

Christ Trump had tremendous business sense, using many little tricks to be successful in his real estate business. It is very interesting that even though Frederick Christ Trump was born in New York City in 1905 from German origins, from World War II until the 1980s, Fredrick used to tell friends and acquaintances that he was from a Swedish background. John Walter, his nephew and the Trump family historian, explained, "He had a lot of Jewish tenants and it wasn't a good thing to be German in those days." It worked perfectly for the Jewish tenants as well as for Trump.

Their business was growing steadily, and one of the things Christ Trump did with his earnings, as his sons said, was to help send his younger son John Trump to Brooklyn Polytechnic Institute, then to Columbia for his master's and then to the Massachusetts Institute of Technology, where he received his Ph.D.

When he started at Brooklyn Polytechnic, John Trump was planning to become an architect and to go into the real estate business with his brother Fred. "The two actually built one or two homes together," Walter said, "but before long, they realized they had two very different philosophies."

"They laughed about it together later," their nephew said. "John designed the house, and before it was finished, Fred wanted to sell it; you know, that's what you do when you're in real estate. But John was a scientist; he wanted to wait until it was totally done. After about a year, my uncle John switched to electrical engineering, was not interested in building design anymore." His other brother Fred soon became an alcoholic.

Donald Trump had the perfect opportunity to hold the reign of their family business while his mother was still writing checks and his father was the Chairman of the Trump Organization. He was a young man in an older-man's business, he had lot of real estate experience and an inexorable thirst for success and fortune.

It happened because his father strongly influenced him to make a career in real estate development, but the younger man's personal goals were much grander than those of his father's. In 1971 Trump moved his residence to Manhattan, where he became familiar with many influential people. Being convinced of the economic opportunity in the city, Trump became involved in large building projects in Manhattan that would offer opportunities for earning high profits, utilizing attractive architectural design, and winning public recognition.

He understood that real estate has to be a show business. From concrete and wood, he moved to sparkling velvet and chromes. Rich people began to buy and the Fifth Street soon became Trump Estate, and Trump trumped New York during the next two decades. He became Mr. Trump, the Real Estate Mogul of New York.

On the other hand, his alcoholic brother Fred Trump Jr. died at the age of 42 in 1981. His death had far-reaching impact on Donald Trump, resulting in his abstinence from alcohol, smoking and drugs.

"He was a great guy, a handsome person. He was the life of the party. He was a fantastic guy, but he got stuck on alcohol," says Trump, 69. "And it had a profound impact and ultimately [he] became an alcoholic and died of alcoholism. He would tell me, 'Don't drink ever'...He understood the problem that he had and that it was a very hard problem."

Trump met a Czech model in Montreal in 1977 and married her, now named Ivana Zelnicek Trump. Their marriage lasted from 1977-1990. She was not a US citizen. It took 10 long years for her to get US citizenship. They divorced, after three children together: Tiffany, Donald Jr. and Eric Barton.

Then Donald married Marla Maples in 1993 and divorced her in 1999, with huge publicity.

His third and the last marriage took place in 2005, to Melania Knauss. Born on April 26, 1970 in Slovenia, Melania Knauss began her modeling career at the age of sixteen in her own country. At the age of eighteen, she signed with a modeling agency in Milan. After graduating in design and architecture at University in Slovenia, Melania was attending photo shoots in Paris and Milan, and finally she settled in New York in 1996. At 5 feet 11 inches, Melania Trump has a captivating presence in front of the camera.

This marriage must be working fine, since Donald has not made any indication that he is divorcing her.

Donald Trump, the father of five and grandfather of eight, has told PEOPLE Magazine he also impressed the importance of abstaining from drugs and alcohol on his children. "I think they drink a little bit, but not much. But I say no drugs, no alcohol, no cigarettes."

Trump told PEOPLE Magazine for his cover story that his family has always been the most important thing in his life. "I always prided myself on being a good father," he said. "With my children, I was always available."

The Sources of His Fortune

In March 2011 *Forbes Magazine* estimated Donald Trump's net worth to be $2.7 billion, with a $60 million salary. But, in 2015, according to its ranking of the wealthiest people in the U.S., *Forbes Magazine* listed Trump's riches at $4.5 billion. Many praise and analyze his "success" as if it were self-made, and they fail to attribute the proper credit to others where deserved.

Trump's net worth has proved to be a sensitive subject, leading him to file a lawsuit in 2006 against a reporter, who Trump claimed understated his wealth. The lawsuit was eventually dismissed.

Despite what Trump claims as his success as a businessman, it would not have been possible without the contribution from his father, the general public, and the US government. Unfortunately, Trump decided to forget or intentionally and selectively ignore these truths while forming his political philosophy, a sentiment made particularly clear during his brief bid for the 2012 Republican presidential nomination.

1. Inheritance

Some critics say Donald Trump is rich because his father, the real estate mogul in New York Fredrick Christ Trump, was rich. The short answer is that this played a role. His father, and grandfather, have defined the current candidate for president more than anything else, raising the bar by a family culture of doing whatever it takes to come out on top and never giving up.

While Donald Trump inherited wealth from his father, he is personally responsible for accumulating the great bulk of his fortune. Trump's father had a net wealth estimated at between $250 million and $400 million at the time of his death, but had four surviving heirs. Had he invested his inheritance in a managed fund, he'd have got a few billion dollars more until now given that he didn't lose money in some of his business deals and in one of his divorces.

2. Government funding and other money

Government funding and money from other sources helped Christ Trump build his own empire in the early stage of his business, which grew at a staggering rate. In 1934, while struggling during the Great Depression, lucrative financing from the Federal Housing Administration (FHA) allowed Donald Trump's father to revive his business and start building a multitude of homes in Brooklyn, selling at $6,000 apiece. Furthermore, throughout WWII, Fred Trump constructed

FHA-backed housing for US naval personnel near major shipyards along the East Coast.

Decades later, Donald Trump eventually found himself in serious financial trouble. In 1990, due to excessive leveraging, The Trump Organization revealed to the Press that it was $5 billion in debt ($8.8 billion by some estimates), with $1 billion personally guaranteed by Donald Trump himself. The survival of the company was made possible only by a bailout pact agreed upon in August of that same year by some 70 banks, allowing Trump to defer on nearly $1 billion in debt, as well as to take out second and third mortgages on almost all of his properties. If it were not for the collective effort of all these banks and parties involved in that 1990 deal, Trump's business would have gone bankrupt and failed.

Donald Trump made his Trump Hotels & Casino Resorts Inc. public in 1995, and accumulated a substantial financial boost from society and the Securities and Exchange Commission (SEC) regulations in New York that enables the market to function. At the initial stage of this phase, Trump sold 10 million shares at $14 per share and then again in 1996 sold 13.25 million shares at $32.50 a share. This initial public offering granted Trump's company a stability and legitimacy that would have been impossible without millions of people around the world trusting his organization and investing with the hope of shared success.

Despite the clear societal and governmental assistance described above, Trump continues to be outspoken in his criticism of government. In his famous book *The America We Deserve,* Trump explains that "the greatest threat to the American Dream is the idea that dreamers need close government scrutiny and control. Job one for us is to make sure the public sector does a limited job, and no more."

This quote proves to be particularly ironic when considering Trump's feelings about eminent domain laws. He was quoted as saying, "I happen to agree with it 100 percent" when speaking of the 2005 Supreme Court decision on *Kolo v. New London,* which affirmed the government's ability to transfer land from one private owner to another for the purpose of economic development in the area. In fact, Trump attempted to take advantage of eminent domain laws on several occasions, once even demanding that an elderly widow sell her home to his business so that he could build a limousine parking lot.

But more disturbing and hurting than his hypocritical condemnation of the US government is Donald Trump's failure to acknowledge anyone's contributions in the creation of his financial success.

Rather, at the Conservative Political Action Conference at 2011, Trump made clear his feelings on the creation of his fortunes in front of spectators. He strongly said with pride, "Over the years I've participated in many battles and have really almost come out very, very victorious every single time. I've beaten many people and companies, and I've won many wars. I have fairly but intelligently earned many billions of dollars, which in a sense was both a scorecard and acknowledgment of my abilities."

Furthermore, Trump apparently sees no benefit in supporting taxes to maintain institutions such as the Securities and Exchange Commission to regulate the stock market, in which he publicly trades his company and made his business survive off bankruptcy, or the court system, which actively protects his property rights: "We are the highest taxed nation— I would tax foreign countries that are ripping off the US, and lower taxes for Americans." He has no gratitude either for the SEC or the government. When their job is done, all the credit goes to him.

Trump was born with a golden spoon, being set up for success since his birth. The large inherited wealth left to him by his father, the experience he was provided in his early years in real estate, coupled with the contributions and the protections of society and the US government made his ascension to the Forbes 400 list almost inevitable. But Trump fails to recognize these facts and continues expressing his belief that he did it all alone.

3. His business accomplishments

Donald Trump is a successful businessman despite all criticism. In 1974, he became president of his father's organization. During the 15 years following his ascension to the top of the hierarchy, he single-handedly expanded the corporation, buying and branding buildings, golf courses, hotels, casinos, and other recreational facilities. In 1980 he established The Trump Organization to oversee all of his real estate operations.

As soon as he became the president of his father's business, Trump obtained an Option on one of the Penn Central's hotels, the Commodore, which was unprofitable but in an excellent location near Grand Central Station. The next year, he signed a partnership agreement with the Hyatt Hotel Corporation, which did not have a large downtown hotel. Trump then worked out a complicated deal with the city to revamp the hotel. Renamed the Grand Hyatt, the hotel was popular and an economic success. This was his first milestone as the president of the organization. It gained his father's approval and made Trump the city's best known and most controversial real estate developer. This was the beginning of his journey through accomplishments, branding, glamor and fame.

When the Pennsylvania Central Railroad entered bankruptcy, Trump was able to obtain an Option (a contract that gives a person the authority to sell something for a specific price during a limited time frame) on the railroad's yards on the west side of Manhattan.

Right after that, when plans for apartments were refused because of a poor economic climate, Trump promoted the property as the location of a city convention center, and the city government selected it over two other sites in 1978. Trump's offer to drop a fee if the center were named after his family, however, was turned down, along with his bid to build the complex.

In 1979, Trump rented a site on Fifth Avenue next to the famous Tiffany & Company as the location for a monumental $200 million apartment-retail complex designed by Der Scutt. It was named Trump Tower when it opened in 1982. The fifty-eight-story building featured a six-story courtyard lined with pink marble, and included an eighty-foot waterfall. The luxurious building attracted well-known retail stores and celebrity renters and brought Trump national attention.

Meanwhile, Trump was investigating in the profitable casino gambling business, which was approved in New Jersey in 1977. In 1980, he was able to acquire a piece of property in Atlantic City, New Jersey. He brought in his younger brother Robert to head up the complex project of acquiring the land, winning a gambling license, and obtaining permits and financing. Holiday Inns Corporation, the parent company of Harrah's casino hotels, offered a partnership, and the $250 million complex opened in 1982 as Harrah's at Trump Plaza. Trump bought out Holiday Inns in 1986 and renamed the facility Trump Plaza Hotel and Casino. Trump also purchased a Hilton Hotels casino-hotel in Atlantic City when the corporation failed to obtain a gambling license, and renamed the $320 million complex Trump's Castle. Later, while it was under construction, he was able to acquire the largest hotel-casino in the world, the Taj Mahal at Atlantic City, which opened in 1990.

Back in New York City, Trump purchased an apartment building and the Barbizon-Plaza Hotel, which faced Central Park, with plans to build a large condominium tower on the site. The tenants of the apartment building, however, who were protected by the city's rent control and rent stabilization programs, fought Trump's plans and won in the Court of Law. Trump then renovated the Barbizon, renaming it Trump Parc. In 1985, he purchased seventy-six acres on the west side of Manhattan for $88 million to build a complex to be called Television City, which was to consist of a dozen skyscrapers, a mall, and a riverfront park. The huge development was to stress television production, and feature the world's tallest building, but community opposition and a long city approval process delayed construction of the project. In 1988 he acquired the Plaza Hotel for $407 million and spent $50 million renovating it under his then wife Ivana's direction.

It was not until 1990, however, that the real estate market declined, reducing the value of and income from Trump's empire; his own net worth plummeted from an estimated $1.7 billion to $500 million. The Trump Organization required massive loans to keep it from collapsing, a situation that raised troubling questions as to whether the corporation could survive bankruptcy. Some observers saw Trump's decline as symbolic of many of the business, economic, and social excesses from the 1980s.

Yet Trump climbed back and was reported to be worth close to $2 billion in 1997. Donald Trump's image was tarnished by the publicity surrounding his controversial separation and the later divorce from his wife, Ivana. But Trump married again, this time to Marla Maples, a fledgling actress. The couple had a daughter two months before their marriage in 1993. He filed for a highly publicized divorce from Maples in 1997, which became final in June 1999.

On October 7, 1999, Trump announced the formation of an exploratory committee to inform his decision of whether he should seek the Reform Party's nomination for the presidential race of 2000, but backed out because of problems within the party.

A state appeals court ruled on August 3, 2000 that Trump had the right to finish an 856-foot-tall condominium on New York City's east side. The Coalition for Responsible Development had sued the city, charging it with violation of zoning laws by allowing the building to reach heights that towered over everything in its neighborhood. The city authority had since moved to revise its rules to prevent more such projects. However, his opponents couldn't stop him. They failed to obtain an injunction (a court order to stop), and so allowed him to continue construction.

He has created a system where his money is re-invested at compounded rates, and he has created a system where others are interested in re-investing money in his system, to make money for Trump and for themselves. This is branding. Trump and other investors are investing and reinvesting in his branding and making money for all parties. His good-will, business branding - a unique money-making machine, and charisma as a Celebrity have made him so famous.

Who Are Trump's Followers?

Who are Donald Trump's voters? And his followers? Trump has created voters for himself by attracting disaffected and indifferent Republican voters, iffy or confused give-me-a-sensational-hard-poke-on-my-head-I-will-hear-you-sir type of people, and people who don't normally vote, but now intend to support him. Last of all, his provocative, realistic, people-like-to-hear type of entertaining statements have turned his so-so followers into voters. This is a great achievement for a real estate tycoon who has been smashing all the seasoned and smooth politicians within the establishment of the Republican Party. He started his business career with concrete and wood, then velvet and chrome, now with provocative and derogatory comments.

Trump's Muslim-ban idea or comment is supported by two-thirds of likely GOP primary voters, based on a New Hampshire poll, Bloomberg.com reports.

A RealClearPolitics.com report shows that Trump has the support of 30.4 percent of GOP voters nationwide, when averaging the most recent polls. That is almost double the second place holder in the GOP.

All of these unexpected political achievements raise the question, who are these people who support Trump so blindly? Who are buying his vicious, propagandizing, inflammatory remarks? Records from various media and polling firms show that these sections of the electorate are disaffected, tend to be Republican, and are mostly but not entirely white, poorly educated, and became indifferent to the Republican Party and politics during the Obama tenure.

And most importantly, according to focus groups led by Frank Luntz, a top Republican pollster cited by the *Washington Post* and *Wall Street Journal*, these voters have become incredibly loyal to Trump, supportive of his posturing and swipes, and completely unmoved by condemnations of their candidate from world leaders around the globe. After all, America is the strongest sanctuary of these extremists.

In the *Washington Post*, Luntz is quoted as saying, "I've never seen anything like this. There is no sign of them leaving." In *Journal*, he registers six features of Trump's supporters:

1. They have a dim view of the U.S.
2. They hate President Barack Obama
3. They hate the media, too
4. They are suspicious of Muslims

5.   They are unswervingly loyal to Trump
6.   They kind of like Texas Sen. Ted Cruz.

The *Los Angeles Times*, in a recent diagnostic analysis of its polling data, discovers that Trump supporters increase with age. Only 15 percent are aged 18 to 29; 53 percent are aged 30 to 64; and 34 percent are 65 and older.

Many voters and supporters, who participated in the poll, did not state their race, but of those who did,

1.   Thirty-one percent said they were white
2.   Twelve percent said they were black
3.   Eleven percent said Latino.

And they span the economic spectrum as follows:

1.   Twenty-eight percent said they made less than $50,000 a year.
2.   The same percentage said they made between $50,000 and $100,000.
3.   Twenty-two percent said they made more than $100,000. This data was from the November, 25, 2015 poll.

The most detailed analysis might be from RealClearPolitics.com, which investigated the personalities of people who would be drawn to Trump's presence. His supporters are not particularly ideological, but mostly in the Republican camp. Only "20 percent of his supporters describe themselves as 'liberal' or 'moderate.'" They're also "a bit older, less educated and earn less than the average Republican. Slightly over half are women."

On education, "One half of his voters have a high school education or less, compared to 19 percent with a college or post-graduate degree," the website's reporters said, adding that Trump appeals to a certain breed of southern Re-publican, especially in Texas. "The Donald appears to have a special appeal to Texans: he took the highest proportion of support from Ted Cruz, then from Rick Perry," the former governor who slammed Trump before withdrawing from the race. "Trumpism—a toxic mix of demagoguery and nonsense."

The *New York Times*, when analyzing the content and style of the 95,000 words comprising all of Trump's speeches in the five months between July and November 2015, quoted saying that his "pattern of elevating emotional appeals over rational ones is a rhetorical style that historians, psychologists and political scientists placed in the tradition of political figures like Barry Goldwater, George Wallace, Joseph McCarthy, Huey Long and Pat Buchanan, who used fiery language to try to win the favor with struggling or scared Americans."

These analysts compare Trump to some of America's worst demagogues. "Several historians watched Mr. Trump's speeches for months, at the request of the *Times*, and observed techniques, like vilifying groups of people and stoking the insecurities of his audiences, that they associate with Wallace and McCarthy."

He is not spending so much money for campaign ads because he has already got enough free exposure on TV and social media attention. Trump has struck pay dirt with KKK, xenophobes and racists, who have found a hero – one who speaks of their beliefs. His character is like a George Orwellian villain—who is well on his way to winning the office of the President of the United States.

Trump knows the German style of propaganda, which is demagoguery. As his political campaign for the presidency continues advancing, the world will not be surprised if he will be, like Adolf Hitler, controlling and commanding a 21st-century American version of the "good Germans," people who are seduced by his pervading boasts, prejudice, blame-games, war-mongering and untouchable-authoritative attitude. As

Gustave Gilbert, the prison psychiatrist at the post-WWII Nuremburg War Crimes Tribunal once made a famous quote, "The perpetrators showed no great deviation from the norm."

Trump's such attitude and Frankenstein style will create a new world-order.

On January 29, 2016, at a campaign rally, Trump made the claim that "I could stand in the middle of 5th Avenue and shoot somebody and I wouldn't lose voters."

Even though Trump announced his candidacy in Mid-2015, current political conditions in the US have matured for a serious Trump candidacy in the year of 2016. His well-branded combination of big promises and low-attitude gesturing at threats from Mexican rapists and Syrian refugees has rekindled hope in the hearts of disaffected and indifferent Republicans, and fear in the hearts of everyone else, including the leadership of his own party. Against all odds, and despite all the negative predictions by his die-hard critics—Trump has remained stubbornly atop Republican primary polls. Frightened and suspicious Americans are buying his message. Their anti-intellectualism is one of the greatest assets for Trump and his branding to exercise his word-cannibalism in a depraved American society.

Miguel de Unamuno said, "That which the fascists hate above all else, is intelligence." And fascists are successful politicians for a time being.

Trump always has a unique mix of sensationalism and controversy to attract the media's interest and attention like holding a megaphone and screaming through it with fun and tricks. And his capture of the media is more important to a fascist than marching millions of para-military on the streets of America. Democracy is helpless and severely incompetent at this moment.

"I play to people's fantasies," Trump writes. "People may not always think big themselves, but they can still get very excited by those who do. That's why a little hyperbole never hurts. People want to believe that something is the biggest and the greatest and the most spectacular."

Scarily, one passionate and dedicated Trump supporter who was paranoid by Trump's fiery-brilliance in demagoguery said, "A resounding applause to you, Herr Trump. And please pay no mind to the anti-White idiots insulting you."

Trump's Branding

Branding is a marketing strategy that involves creating a differentiated name and image – often using a logo or a tag line, in order to establish a presence in the consumer's mind and attract and retain existing customers. Donald Trump's branding sign is the word TRUMP.

Trump's brand is used for the reflexive production of symbolic values and lifestyle. Then gradually the brands, his trope and his high level of self-marketing have made his branding unique among the upper and luxury classes in New York and around the world.

Trumps sheer business branding has helped make his organization one of the world's most successful companies that connect with their customers with a significant impact in the long run and make business or deals easier and profitable.

Making deals is his art form, and for this art, he created a unique branding of five big letters as high as a man. The five letters shine on the Fifth Street, a place of Donald Trump's excitement and sensation. People, especially Americans, love it.

Trump's own trump card is his own branding, which has more wins than losses in the harsh capitalist US market.

TRUMP has matured, established, deep-rooted in American society, and successfully sprawling out of America. A Trump building exists almost every city in the USA.

In 1971, Trump moved his residence to Manhattan, where he became familiar with many influential people. Being aware of the economic opportunity in the richest city, Trump became involved in large building projects in booming Manhattan that offered him opportunities for earning high profits, utilizing attractive architectural design, and winning public recognition. This move gave Donald a tremendous exposure to the business community in Manhattan. Since, then, he didn't have any need to move, because he found a place that supported his lifestyle and an opportunity to transform a personal brand, which was built over the generations, to a remarkable business brand, a trademark in New York City.

His location said something stronger about his brand because it reflected his choice, not his company's. This is great news for Trump, who sought a better alignment between work and life. His dream was larger than that of his grandfather during the Klondike Gold Rush. He smelled opportunities and one of the things he realized to be successful in the competitive community is a unique business branding to gain money, wealth, and power. It required a different approach to personal branding to make sure, out of sight is not out of mind.

Trump's personal branding also had a tremendous impact on the real estate market and construction business. This has driven up demand for, and the price of, real estate in desirable locations that were once thought of only as vacation spots, such as beachfront properties with easy access to airports and highways. Trump understood that and began to solidify his branding for his business. Everyone loves the excitement around Trump revealing a new magnificent building, casino or golf course that's being built, either in the US or somewhere in the world.

He has built everything within the framework of branding: from real estate development and brokerage houses to casinos, hotels, golf courses, branded consumer goods ranging from golf clubs, restaurants, an airline, a furniture collection, a menswear label, boxed chocolates, loose leaf teas, vodka, and a slew of books, bottled water, beauty pageants, modeling, a production company, and ice skating rinks. And yes, even a network marketing company, which is now non-operational.

But his journey through the process of branding was not smooth. Trump's ability to successfully use negative messages from his opponents is fascinating, sometimes entertaining, and always catches media attention. Strong brands often deter as much as they attract. And Donald Trump is the master deterrent, a sure winner in the chess game.

Through constant struggle, and the use of various strategies, Trump's brand has been being well-designed and fabricated on an endless effort of his ever-growing number of enemies dating all the way back to the '80s.

In New York, the co-founders of satirical magazine *Spy*, Kurt Andersen and Graydon Carter, put Donald on their regular punch list. *Spy* magazine has been packed with stringent words only for Donald, who became the notorious "short-fingered vulgarian" in their relentless parodies. They used to torment Trump by zeroing in on his many questionable business dealings and his outlandish personal traits that we can see nowadays.

That was a crucial time for the emerging Trump brand. Not many entrepreneurs at that time could handle being a constant punching bag. Trump arduously turned every jab into gold. This is his great success, because that magazine did actually a great job for his publicity and his branding has become a unique example of money and glamor in the US.

Then came the new century with fast-tracking for his branding and business. Global cable channels, Twitter and other social media have immensely improved his branding platform, making Trump's habitual rage a phenomenally famous attribute of his brand. But social media, especially twitter, simply turbo-charged his attribute and business image, a brand that was already built for speed, success and universality.

His branding has paid him back amazingly. His initial financial disclosures with the Federal Election Commission valued his name only at $3,320,020,000, nearly a half of his total worth. That's the value of the goodwill of his organization.

Trump changed the domain of his branding – from business to the highest level of politics – when he announced a full run for candidacy in 2015 with his slogan "Make America Great Again." The Trump brand, transformed from business to politics, is aggressive and all about 'kicking ass' in the marketplace. The brand word 'TRUMP' has become synonymous with success, luxury and being arrogant and fearless. While some may say it's too aggressive, like him or not, you have to respect what he has already accomplished in his political campaign. It is his unique branding, which came from his forefathers, doing it any way and never giving up. That is why he is winning, and stunning his confused critics.

What remains significant is an ideally pure Trumpian endeavor that distorts the line between campaigning and brand-building, and complicates Trump's claims that he is funding his own political campaign. About seventy-five percent of Trump's total campaign spending has either gone to reimburse his own businesses or has been covered by funds from grass-roots donors, according to an analysis of F.E.C. reports by *The New York Times*. Virtually all of the money Mr. Trump himself has put into the campaign was lent, rather than donated outright, meaning that he could potentially sell enough hats and T-shirts to pay himself back down the road. This is the sheer power of his branding.

"I think there's always been a case to be made that Donald Trump looked at this as a way to extend his brand to a new generation of people," said Rick Wilson, a Florida-based Republican strategist who has done work for a group supporting Senator Marco Rubio of Florida. "I bet 'Art of the Deal' was in the remainder bin until this year."

But how does his business branding impact his political campaign so smoothly and successfully? Trump's sheer branding naturally reinforces the central message in his political campaign: "This is a talented and very successful entrepreneur who has earned the right to pass judgment on others' business prowess." This is his basic instinct, after all these years of experience in business. He creates controversy in the media and among the voters through his provocative statements, and by doing so, he opens the gate for his branding for a smooth run. Thus, his business branding made his political gesture so authoritative and provocative to his voters and others in a free Enterprise like the USA.

Trump gives messages to his followers that are consistent, strong, and action-oriented. This technique comes from his captivating branding that has already attracted customers and reinvented his images in the digital world.

It is true that if Trump does become president, his brand will take on a sensational swing. The Oval Office may be forever in the business world and his fortunes will sky-rocket. He will be virtually guaranteed seven-figure booking advances and half-million-dollar speaking arrangements after he leaves the office, as previous White House occupants have proved already given that humanity survives his presidency.

He has deliberately incurred a lot of negative publicity during his political campaign. If he loses and needs to return to civilian life, this may become distinctly unhelpful to his future business endeavors, even though it has made his name recognition almost universal.

Trump will surely retain a large voter base for a while, even if he doesn't win the presidency. But they won't be buying his products at luxury retailers because of their low income, and wealthy real-estate buyers may hesitate to buy a new condo unit bearing his brand name. Shareholders may pull out, causing his empire to collapse.

However, surprisingly, Donald Trump strengthens his brand every time he denounces, bullies, and scolds others, because he has created a world with extensive and speedy media connection. Some assumed this was just part of the lingo he has already developed for *The Apprentice*. This is not correct, because the cutting-edge Trump brand is built on real-world differences and bitterness in a harsh imperial war. It has high resiliency.

To be outright hated and criticized is Donald Trump's campaign strategy, and it is working for both, him and his followers. He has built his political brand on being provocative and attracting scorn. Well, the man who loves to be hated is getting his wish, and it is helping him in his presidential bid. When he announced his candidacy at Trump Tower in New York City, Trump made derogatory comments about Mexican immigrants calling them rapists and drug dealers.

Polls conducted after his announcement show that his popularity has increased significantly. In a CNN/ORC national poll, Trump garnered 12% (up from 3% before his announcement of his candidacy), positioning him in second place for the Republican nomination. Then he was up in Iowa and New Hampshire polls too.

In Iowa (from a Quinnipiac poll, January 26, 2016) he was tied with neurosurgeon Ben Carson for second place. And a Suffolk University poll of New Hampshire GOP voters that was conducted after both Bush's and Trump's presidential announcements had Bush at 14% followed by Trump with 11%.

Trump responded to recent poll results by saying that the numbers are "representative of the response we are receiving from all over the country."

"I am committed to addressing the issues our country is facing and am confident my business mindset and common sense solutions are resonating with the American people," Trump said. "Politicians are all talk and no action and the American public is ready for a leader with a proven track record of success."

In an interview with CNN's Don Lemon, Trump didn't shy away from his controversial comments, saying, "Well, somebody's doing the raping, Don! I mean somebody's doing it! Who's doing the raping? Who's doing the raping?"

He has support from fellow candidate Ted Cruz, who said on Fox News, "I like Donald Trump. I think he's terrific, I think he's brash, I think he speaks the truth and I think NBC is engaging in political correctness that is silly and that is wrong."

But Trump's support from some is nothing compared to the galaxy of denouncements from major brands:

NBC: They severed their ties to Trump, saying, "Due to the recent derogatory statements by Donald Trump regarding immigrants, NBC/Universal is ending its business relationship with Mr. Trump."

The Miss USA and Miss Universe pageants, (part of a joint venture between Trump and NBC), will no longer air on their network.

Univision: Univision, which airs the Miss USA and Miss Universe pageants, stated that they would end their relationship with Trump because of his remarks. This prompted Trump to launch a $500 million lawsuit against Univision.

Macy's: The national retailer announced that they would dump Trump's clothing line. Trump responded by saying he is the one who decided to end the relationship with Macy's.

New York City: Mayor Bill de Blasio said his administration is reviewing the city's business relationships with Donald Trump. One of the partnerships being re-considered is Trump's golf course deal, which involves the Trump Golf Links at Ferry Point in the Bronx. Other deals being reviewed include a skating rink and other real estate.

Trump's recent jump in the polls might be unrelated to his recent remarks about Mexican immigrants. It could be due to his name recognition, and perhaps there is a delay in the response to his comments about immigrants. Time will tell.

Perhaps the biggest issue has nothing to do with Trump at all. How will Donald Trump's comments impact the Republican Party's brand? Will his opinions rub off on the GOP and make a poor relationship with Hispanic voters even worse? Now Muslims? Then the disabled? Will others from the large field of Republican candidates renounce Trump?

We are in the early days of the biting political campaign. There is a lot of potential venom to be spewed, and like Newton's third law, there will always be an equal and opposite reaction.

He used to be a decent businessman, but his political campaign with provocative statements has changed the direction of his brand forever, from one of ambition and wealth to that of hostility, xenophobia and chauvinism. This is the initial stage of a moral collapse in the US Presidential campaign, and possibly of his empire as well.

Trump and Fascism

Trump is deliberately drawing historical parallels for himself. This points to the fact that America is in danger, at a crossroads between Fascism and Democracy.

Political pundits and candidates alike, who understand the Trump risk, are now accusing Trump of being a fascist or neo-Nazi. Some are even comparing him to Adolf Hitler. But this comparison creates a serious problem, not only for Trump, but for the collective intelligence of all Americans, as conscientious and patriotic people.

The Marxist Theorist and revolutionary Rosa Luxemburg once wrote, "Bourgeois society stands at the crossroads, either transition to Socialism or regression into Barbarism."

In 1932, Leon Trotsky correctly predicted that a divided left would strengthen the fascists, and that the fascists would consequently destroy them: "Should fascism come to power, it will ride over [communist] skulls and spines like a terrific tank. Your salvation lies in merciless struggle. And only a fighting unity with the Social Democratic workers can bring victory."

As the Nazis were growing in size and number before Hitler rose to power before the WWII, the German communists made outrageous claims that the Social Democrats in Germany were themselves fascists. That was one of the gravest political errors the German communists made in their history. Within a short period of time, these divisions on the left helped empower the real fascists – the Nazis. The rise of Hitler destroyed both the German communists and the Social Democrats.

Recently, some critics have argued that Trump is heading to a new brand of fascism in the USA, using his very successful business branding. This is scary to the world and to the liberals in the USA. And there is no shortage of arguments to compare Donald Trump to Adolf Hitler.

"America will suffer Weimar-like hyperinflation any day now." This is the warning that has been made by New York Times columnist Paul Krugman over the years, which has no basis in reality. Nobody else has thought that hyperinflation was imminent in USA.

But now the US' biggest problem may be that it is printing too much money, which hurts both the middle class and the poor. The world's biggest economy could enter into hyperinflation, where the value of a dollar is considerably less than it used to be.

The situation in America may not be the new Weimar Republic, and Trump may not be the reincarnation of Hitler, but there are many interesting similarities between them, to see how a modern democratic state can falter to demagoguery in times of extreme economic polarization, and social and racial discontent.

Sadly, America is helplessly divided like the Weimar Republic was, and Trump is running to revive the sinking America to its glory days of the past, a political fantasy. But surely, America is losing democracy.

For many right-wing white Americans, this means going back to the days before immigrants and minorities changed the country's singular-color face, and before the "incompetent," "ineffective" leaders let foreign nations and religions frighten them into helplessness, trauma and then submission. For the fascist Adolf Hitler, it was the Treaty of Versailles, a treaty of submission; for Trump, it is unfair, disadvantageous trade deals with Mexico and China, the nuclear deal with Iran, etc. There is a parallel.

Franklin D. Roosevelt once made a comment on fascism: "If American democracy ceases to move forward as a living force, seeking day and night by peaceful means to better the lot of our citizens, fascism will grow in strength in our land."

Now we can see, many decades later, an increasingly polarized political spectrum backed up by power and money, which has opened the door for Trump's demagoguery and authoritarianism in this political campaign of 2016. The trend is very disturbing in a time of persistent economic downturn, political stagnation and unstoppable inequality.

But what has helped Trump to reach this height? The sense of hopelessness, anger, betrayal and frustration has led white KKKs, supremacist and right-wing groups to make very bad decisions. Every time Trump has given a statement of outrage, his ratings have gone up. Now America's mood is revolutionary.

This trend was initially fueled by the 2008 election of Barack Obama, who sparked, unwillingly and unknowingly, a reaction by the right-wing populists, and now that reaction has become a political backlash for America. And Obama did it not because of his politics and policies but because of his cultural impact, and partly because of his middle name, Hussein.

When Obama was elected, the world congratulated him along with most Americans, and wished him the best. He is a good man. But the world didn't think that the right-wing white populist reaction and sentiments would get this much momentum. This is a naked aggression against US democracy, and the Constitution, and the best spice for ISIS and other Muslim radicals to recruit more: "See how Americans hate us, the Muslims."

Trump's bitter and strategic polarization at a time of crisis continues to enlarge both the differences between the two major US political parties, as well as among different factions within the parties themselves. This is especially so within the Republican Party, which could easily be divided into three or four different parties today. These divisions, like the divisions between the German communists and the German Social Democrats, has created an environment ripe for an extremist like Trump. And even if Trump does not get the nomination, the political, social and media insurgency he has led, and the growing authoritarian impulse and divisions that he has already created within the Republican Party, will have a long lasting impact on American politics and its democratic establishments.

Dmitri Orlov described "the end of the Soviet Union as the lifting of a dream, a sudden realization that what was ludicrous was in fact powerless as well." How Trump wins is by exposing and recognizing this ludicrous unreality in the established "norms" of political behavior and traditions. Trump is neither a full-bloomed typical fascist nor a comedian. He simply gives the failed US political system no more respect than it can actually command in the real world. Against this, the Clintons and the Republican campaigns, can offer only a half-throated reassurance that American rules and traditions aren't bankrupt yet. But Trump followers are not willing to listen to them, because they do not have any faith and respect for any established political norms. Instead, they respond with a deep-throated growl, with anger.

It is undeniably true that millions of liberal American voters are now supporting democratic socialist Jewish Bernie Sanders for President, when millions of right-wing Americans are supporting a provocative man who cheerfully advocates torture, elimination, invasions, and would consider creating a database for certain religious minorities. If the expected change does not come from a united progressive movement that promotes gross economic fairness and wide open social justice, it may just come from a new fascist movement on the extreme right. The Americans are at a crossroads: "Either socialism or barbarism."

Before the rise of fascism under Adolf Hitler, both Germany and Italy were constitutionally liberal democracies.

Fascism did not sweep over these nations as if it were from a different planet, but was their own creation on their own soil. Actually, these countries were still democratic while the fascist dictatorship was rising, due to enormous political and economic changes they went through. In parallel, the US has a liberal democracy now under President Obama, but is moving toward a fascist dictatorship if Trump wins. Fascism worked differently in different countries, and this will be true in the US.

The Southern Poverty Law Center (SPLC) and the Anti-Defamation League (ADL) have already warned the USA that Trump's provocative rhetoric fuels anti-Muslim violence. Violence against the Muslims in the USA will rise and is rising. One Muslim lady was not allowed to attend Trump's "democratic" Republican rally, and another one was shoved out from a meeting with ugly comments. The days of equality in USA are gone. There is a new brand of politics that the KKK likes, White Supremacists like, racists love, anti-Muslim extremists love. And additionally, Trump has created an extreme group against the Hispanics.

Recently, a report appeared in the blog Boing, re-producing an article from a 1927 edition of the *New York Times*. This report suggests that Donald Trump's late father might have had a connection to the Ku Klux Klan.

A man named Fred Christ Trump was among those arrested in a massive brawl between angry KKK members and NY Police at a 1927 Memorial Day parade in New York City, the report said.

Christ Trump's son Donald Trump has raised eye-brows when he refused to disavow Ku Klux Klan grand wizard David Duke's endorsement on CNN's *State of the Union*. He shrugged off having any prior knowledge of the KKK and their message, saying he couldn't disavow Duke's statement as he simply knows "nothing about white supremacists."

As *The Atlantic*'s Yoni Appelbaum pointed out, the Republican front-runner's refusal to repudiate white supremacists' support as well as the bombast in his campaign are both echoes of the Ku Klux Klan.

Trump should be rather knowledgeable about the white supremacist organization, as he has had a tricky past with the KKK before, beginning with his father, Fred Trump.

The *Times* article mentioned the arrestee's address as 175-24 Devonshire Road in Jamaica Estates, Queens. Past local news reports noted that the Republican presidential frontrunner's father used to live at that address. Donald Trump's German immigrant grandfather died nine years before this brawl took place in New York.

While six others arrested in the brawl faced charges, the Times report noted that Fred Christ Trump was discharged. All seven of these men were represented by the same team of two lawyers, according to the *Times* report.

The *Times* reported that New York Police said the brawl broke out because the Klan broke an agreement not to wear any of their symbols to the parade. The Klan members though, for their part, accused the police of going over their authority in trying to keep them out of the peaceful parade.

The elder Trump, Fred Christ Trump, was born in 1905, which would put him in his early '20s when The New York Times covered the brawl. His wife, Mary Anne, didn't give birth to the couple's son Donald until 1946.

Donald Trump's presidential campaign did not immediately respond to Boing Boing's request for comment.

It is unclear to what extent, if any, Fred Crist Trump was involved with the group, based on the New York Times report. As the incident happened nearly 20 years before Donald Trump was born, it's also unclear whether the real estate mogul knew anything of his father's youthful arrest.

Next, the Boston beating incident surprised the world even more. A homeless Hispanic man was lying on the ground, shaking, when police arrived at the scene in Boston. His face was soaked with urine, his nose broken, his chest and arms injured.

Boston Police said two brothers from South Boston ambushed this 58-year-old as he slept outside a Dorchester MBTA stop, and targeted him because he was Hispanic. One of the brothers said he was inspired in part by GOP presidential candidate Donald Trump.

The allegations ignited widespread condemnation for this heinous act and Donald Trump received some of the blame as well.

Republican presidential front-runner Donald Trump said later he "would never condone violence."

"Donald Trump was right," the two men said, according to Boston police, as they beat the man with a metal pipe and then urinated on him. "All these illegals need to be deported."

Trump sincerely tweeted on the following Friday that the incident was "terrible."

Trump said, "We need energy and passion, but we must treat each other with respect."

KKK now uses Trump as a juicy bait in its outreach efforts within the community. Trump is their modern day demigod they have been missing all these decades. This is despite Trump saying that he keeps a distance from them.

Stormfront, the most famous American white supremacist website, has recently upgraded its servers to cope with a Trump traffic rise. Former Louisiana Republican David Duke says that the Trump has given more Americans cover to speak out loud about white nationalism than at any time since his own political campaigns in the 1990s.

The Southern Poverty Law Center (SPLC) and the Anti-Defamation League (ADL) warn that Trump's rhetoric favors anti-Muslim violence. White nationalist leaders are capitalizing on his candidacy to invigorate and expand their movement.

Interestingly, Trump doesn't belong to or endorse any white supremacist groups. He has said that he does not need or want Duke's endorsement, and his campaign has fired two staffers over racist posts on social media. A man displaying a Confederate flag was ejected from a Trump rally in Virginia earlier this month.

Actually, Trump's rise directly resonates with the 1920s KKK, the same provocative rhetoric, racist in nature and anti-immigrant.

Therefore, white supremacist leaders consistently say that Trump's rhetoric about the minority groups (Muslims, Hispanics, Blacks, and disabled) has successfully simmered in rising racial resentments long ignored by mainstream politicians, even by President Obama. Trump has shed more light on their agenda than any American political figure has in decades. Trump's rise is a development many of them see as a golden opportunity.

According to the experts at the Anti-Defamation League (ADL) and the Southern Poverty Law Center (SPLC), Trump's call to halt the entry of Muslims to the United States is driving online chatter among white supremacists and is likely to inspire violence against Muslims.

"When well-known public figures make these kinds of statements in the public square, they are taken as a permission-giving by criminal elements who go out and act on their words," said Mark Potok of the SPLC. "Is it energizing the groups? Yeah! They are overly thrilled."

Marilyn Mayo, co-director of the ADL's Center on Extremism, said Trump's proposal to halt the entrance of Muslims into the United States is only the latest statement to inject vigor into the racist fringe of American politics. "Since the beginning of Donald Trump's candidacy, we've definitely seen that a segment of the white supremacist movement, from racist intellectuals to neo-Nazis have been energized," she said.

A spokeswoman for the Trump campaign did not respond to requests for comment.

However, Don Black of Stormfront has admitted that Trump's rhetoric has been a great advantage to white nationalists and populists. "He has sparked an insurgency and I don't think it's going to go away," he told POLITICO.

Rachel Pendergraft, a spokeswoman for the Arkansas-based Knights Party, which considers itself the national standard-bearer for the KKK, said the group encourages its members to engage with their communities through political volunteer work and, at the right moment, steer conversation toward race and "white genocide."

Trump, she said, has offered KKK members a prime opportunity to feel out potential recruits on their racial attitudes and agenda. "Right now he is a major talking point. He is in the news a lot."

Duke, a former grand wizard of the KKK, said Trump, a successful businessman and the subject of nonstop media coverage, has given Americans license to more openly voice their racial hatred.

"He's made it OK to talk about these incredible concerns of European Americans today, because I think European Americans know they are the only group that can't defend their own essential interests and their point of view," Duke said. "He's meant a lot for the human rights of European Americans."

Even those white supremacists who remain unconvinced that Trump is one of them welcome his entrance to the political arena. "As long as he's causing chaos and havoc with the citizens, he's fine with me," said former KKK leader Tom Metzger, founder of the racial separatist group White Aryan Resistance. "I love it."

People who have studied in depth the extremist right in US history as a sociopolitical phenomenon are acutely aware of a simple truth: America has been very, very lucky so far when it comes to fascistic political movements and their rise to the power. The movements have not destroyed American democratic institutions yet.

And now, with the arrival of the Donald Trump 2016 phenomenon that luck may be running out.

This phenomenon, mostly fascist in nature, is not just a fluke. Trump is the logical end result of an endless series of aggressions, on not just American liberalism, but on democratic institutions. The American right-wing is not a detached social phenomenon. Rather, for many years, it has solidly been backed by the broadcast media. It is the long-term plan and struggle of radicalization of the right-wing, and Trump, most probably, is at the end of that struggle for now.

Interestingly, fascistic elements and tendencies have always been part of democratic America. It has been hidden, and occasionally surfaced. Indeed, the worst traits of fascism in Europe were borrowed from American models, particularly eliminationist tendencies, manifested first in the form of racial and ethnic segregation, and ultimately in genocidal violence against the Native Americans.

Adolf Hitler admired the American genocide against Native Americans, as well as the segregationist policies of the Jim Crow regime in the South (which the Nuremberg Race Laws were modeled on), and the threat of the lynch mob embodied in the Ku Klux Klan.

Nazi racial beliefs of the superiority of an Aryan master race arose from earlier proponents of a supremacist conception of race, now-a-days, we can see in America, in the white supremacist fringes. According to Ernst Hanfstaengl, a German business-man and intimate friend of Adolf Hitler before falling out of favor and defecting from Germany, Hitler was "passionately interested in the Ku Klux Klan. ... He seemed to think it was a political movement similar to his own." And indeed it was.

Even though the long-running presence of these elements have been in very American social mosaic, American people has never yet paved the way to fascism, even to proto-fascism. Most probably, this is because the Americans have learned from the wars they fought for freedom and liberty, the end result of segregation and eliminationism (gassing the Jews). And they are appalled by them.

The study of fascism in America has found a few things:

1. Fascism is an historical phenomenon
2. It is current
3. It can be based on the past
4. It could remain dormant
5. It is both complex and simple
6. It resembles a dynamic human psychological pathology
7. It is comprised of a galaxy of complex traits that are interconnected in American society
8. The traits rise and fall as it goes through the different development stages with different variations and complexities.
9. These traits can spark organized violence in different ways when they are nurtured in a true fashion.
10. It has never had a national leader to lead people across America
11. It gets full media attention and coverage.

America's current hyperinflation, high rate of unemployment, rising debts, social discontent, racial segregation, the rise of a President of color for two terms, Islamophobia, and wealth polarization are the symptoms that create a perfect ground for American right-wing populists to activate dormant fascism, and nurture it.

That's where Trump comes in, blowing a trumpet to catch media attention.

In many ways, Trump's presidential campaign fills in many important components of real fascism. One of them is that he has filled the role of fascist leader that has been unfilled for many years. Americans have been simply lucky not to have one in the past.

But now, that luck is hanging in the balance. America has found a blooming fascist leader in Donald Trump, who has no background or history as a fascist or a white supremacist or proto-fascist, nor does he express their views and ideologies.

Actually, Trump has successfully owned dormant fascist tendencies in American political arteries without a para-military force, some of it clearly white supremacism, while the majority of it is the structural racism and white privilege that springs from the nation's extensive and fast-growing white-supremacist historical foundations seen in several occasions in the span of the last 200 years.

Senator Huey Long said, "Fascism will come to America in the name of anti-fascism. I'm afraid, based on my own long experience, fascism will come to America in the name of national security."

It is all happening now on behalf of Trump. For his own vested interest, Trump is happily leading Americans down the path toward a fascist state even without being a genuine fascist himself yet. He avoids that because he doesn't want to risk unending harm to his business branding, and eventually the fall of his empire.

Then, is Trump a sort of real fascist in the making? The interesting thing in American political reality is that Trump is neither a white supremacist nor a bona fide fascist himself yet, but it does not make him any less dangerous for the Muslims, the Mexicans, the Blacks, the Hispanics and the disabled. Recently, people have begun to finally use the word 'fascism' in describing Trump's political campaign, and this tendency is rising fast. They urge for something unique to stop fascism on American soil. And there is no doubt that America is sinking, and Trump is winning with a clear strategy into a newborn American fascist sentiment.

These political observers have a reasonable and acceptable point, because Trump has recently met so many of the key components that collectively define genuine fascism – a new-born American fascism.

And while it's true that, as Political Scientist Josh Marshall suggests, "There really is no single, agreed-upon definition of fascism, there's also no doubt that we can grasp the idea of fascism not just by studying its history, but also by examining the various attempts at understanding and defining just what comprises fascism. And in doing so, we can recognize exactly what it is that Trump is doing." Fascism is not only what the fascist leaders say, it is also about what they do.

Fascism, in reality, is a much more complex phenomenon – first it is social, then political and economic. But it starts with contempt and hatred for the weak ones at a social level.

Harald Oftstad's *Our Contempt for Weakness: Nazi Norms and Values - And Our Own* (1989) clarifies the logical extension of the Darwinian struggle against the "lesser" that permeates so much fascist literature: the deep-seated hatred and contempt in which all persons deemed "weaker" (be this ethnic, racial, medical, genetic, or otherwise) are held, and the desire to eliminate them entirely that it fuels.

During Stalin's days, a formula became communist orthodoxy for half a century: "Fascism is the open, terroristic dictatorship of the most reactionary, most chauvinist, and most imperialist elements of finance capital."

Roger Griffin, in his book, defines fascism as "Modern political ideology that seeks to regenerate the social, economic and cultural life of a country by basing it on a heightened sense of national belonging or ethnic identity."

In the past, fascism rejected liberal and democratic ideas such as freedom and individual rights, often pressed for the destruction of elections, legislatures, and other elements of democracy. Despite the boastful idealistic goals of fascism, attempts to build fascist societies have led to wars and persecutions that caused the death of millions of weak ones. In Hitler's case, they were Jews who were weak and needed to be eliminated. In Trump's case, the weak ones are Muslims, Hispanics, disabled and Blacks. Hitler used force. At this stage Trump is using white populist voters to do the same. Trump's fascism is strongly associated with right-wing fanaticism, racism, totalitarianism, and violence, but with no paramilitary force yet.

In Hitler's own words: "The stronger must dominate and not blend with the weaker, thus searching his own greatness. Only the born weakling can view this as cruel, but he after all is only a weak and limited man; for if this law did not prevail, any conceivable higher development of organic living beings would be unthinkable."

"[We will try to] 'save' even the weakest and most sickly at any price, and this plants the seed of a future generation which must inevitably grow more and more deplorable the longer this mockery of Nature and her will continues. [*Mein Kampf – My Struggle* by Adolf Hitler]

If we take a careful look at Trump's political campaign, we will find the fascist traits posing threats to American democracy:

1.   Hitler tried for a decade to eliminate the Jews because he convinced the German nation that Jews were weak

and a threat to their national purity, valor and glory. Now, the same eliminationist rhetoric is the focal point of Trump's political campaign promising to establish a country for Anglo-Saxon Americans. His opening salvo in the campaign, the one that first skyrocketed him to the forefront in the race, poll-wise, and proved wildly popular with Republican voters, was his vow to deport all 12 million of the United States' undocumented immigrants and to erect a high wall on the nation's southern border. Significantly, the language he used to justify such plans calling those immigrants "criminals," "killers," and "rapists," and contending that they bring crime and disease – is a classic rhetoric designed to demonize an entire class of people by reducing them to objects fit only for elimination. Hitler did the same to the Jews.

Trump's political goal is about forming a "purer" community in modern America, and this campaign has been relentless and extensive: When an audience member asked him at a town-hall-style appearance when and how he was going to "get rid of all the Muslims," he responded that "we're going to be looking at a lot of different things."

He now also claims that, if elected, he will send back all the refugees from Syria who have arrived in the United States: "If I win, they're going back," he told one of his approval-roaring campaign crowds. And shortly before he encouraged a crowd that "maybe should have roughed up" a Black Lives Matter protester, he told an interviewer that the movement, Black Lives Matter, is "looking for trouble." Most recently, he tweeted a graphic taken from a neo-Nazi website purporting to demonstrate falsely that black people commit the most murders in America, though he later claimed that he hadn't endorsed the graphic.

The eliminationism initiatives and precedents of Nazi Germany before the WWII became a second 'license' that empowered fascist regimes across Europe to carry out their own eliminationist projects with diminished accountability and political freedom. Finally, this "license," enhanced by the actions of fascists and the collapse of law and order caused by WWII, released politicians, individuals and communities from the burden of legal and moral accountability, turning them into perpetrators of the widest, most brutal, and devastating genocidal campaign that Europe had ever experienced.

2. Donald Trump expresses an ultra-nationalist, extreme right-wing political and economic agenda. After the race-baiting and the ethnic fear-mongering tactics, this is the most obviously fascistic component of Trump's presidential election campaign, embodied in those trucker hats proclaiming: "Make America Great Again." He likes to make America great again for Anglo-Saxon European Americans, attracting emotional, right wing votes regardless of their color and race. Trump himself puts it this way: "The silent majority is back, and we're going to take the country back. We're going to make America great again." This is a pure Hitler's political philosophy that he used to preach in 1934-1938 Germany, enticing and strengthening the German extremists.

Trump's arrogance is a symbol of the myth of the phoenix-like rebirth from the ashes of an entire society to its "golden age." He likes to create a new society of Anglo-Saxon European Americans that we watched in "Mississippi Burning."

3. Trump's deep contempt is not just for liberalism, which provides most of the fuel for his xenophobic rants, particularly against the media, but also for establishments of conservatism. Trump's biggest fan, Rush Limbaugh, boasts: "In parlaying this outsider status of his, he's better at playing the insiders' game than they are, and they are insiders. He's running rings around all of these seasoned, lifelong, highly acclaimed professionals in both the consultant class, the adviser class, the strategist class, and the candidate class. And he's doing it simply by being himself."

4. Trump constantly states America to be in a state of crisis that has made it "the laughingstock" of the rest of the world, and proclaims that this has occurred because of the failures of primarily liberal politicians.

Trump's contempt for weakness is manifested practically every day on the campaign trail, ranging from his disrespecting of former GOP presidential candidate John McCain, a former prisoner of war, as "not a hero" because "I like people who weren't captured," to his recent mockery of a New York Times reporter with a disability.

Again Trump is pointing to the weakness, then to a stronger, violent, puristic society of his own in the name of Anglo-Saxon Europeans.

5. Trump himself embodies the fascist insistency upon male leadership by a man of destiny. His refusal to acknowledge factual evidence of the falsity of many of his proclamations and comments creates a perfect propaganda strategy based on German propaganda specialist Joseph Goebels. A fascist has no remorse, no acknowledgement of falsity.

6. Trump has a war-mongering attitude: in his book "Make America Great Again" he said how Obama's administration has crippled the US military and thus crippled America.

Nazi Hermann Goering said, "Why, of course the people don't want war... That is understood. But, after all, it is the leaders of the country who determine the policy and it is always a simple matter to drag the people along, whether it is a democracy, or a fascist dictatorship, or a parliament, or a communist dictatorship. Voice or no voice, the people can always be brought to the bidding of the leaders. That is easy. All you have to do is tell them they are being attacked, and denounce the peacemakers for lack of patriotism and exposing the country to danger. It works the same in any country."

Trump is not actively involved in violence, but does advocate violence in the form of revolution through the fast and mighty media. He was not happy with the US Electorate College, which allowed Obama to run in 2012. He was ranting at Obama's re-election win on November 7, 2012. Donald Trump, through his tweets, urged for violence, which is a phenomenon of fascism.

1st tweet: "This election is a total sham and a travesty. We are not a democracy."

2nd tweet: "More votes equals a loss...revolution."

3rd tweet: "Let's fight like hell and stop this great and disgusting injustice! The world is laughing at us."

4th tweet: "We can't let this happen. We should march on Washington and stop this travesty. Our nation is totally divided!"

5th tweet: "He lost the popular vote by a lot and won the election. We should have a revolution in this country!"

Here, Trump has not only called for violence, but also has used the emotion and anger of the lowest common denominator of American electorates for his own agenda while selling America to violence and fascism. It also helps us understand why Trump is an extraordinarily dangerous right-wing populist demagogue, and not a genuine, in-the-gene fascist yet. A serious fascist would have called upon not just the crowd to respond with violence, but also his paramilitary allies to respond with retaliatory strikes. Trump didn't do that for few reasons:

1. There is still not much social chaos, or attempts to overpower US Law Enforcements, and Trump has no paramilitary force yet.

2. He has different a tactic: instead of bloodshed, he prefers non-violent, non-active provocation and hatred with psychological impact on his followers and the neutral ones through the media channels. It is like fat in the meat: no one can remove this fascism from the US mainstream.

3. He may be nervous of the fall of his own empire, which could be a consequence of his fascism.

He is not really a pure ideologue but acting out of a firm faith to a consistent worldview, the center point of attention, as all fascists do. Trump's only real ideology is the praise of himself, for his business, for his intended presidency, and he will do and say anything that appeals to the lowest common denominator of the American electorate in order to attract their support − a large right-wing populist segment that breathes and lives on fear, paranoia, hatred and ignorance.

Because of his dormant ideology, Trump could not show any political compromise on November 7, 2012 when Obama won his second term, being someone who respects and knows how to use the democratic process. Above all, Trump does not care for democratic principles, because he knows what he is looking for and how much it is achievable by advancing them. The decline of the American election campaign really started here.

Trump has not expressed a political vision. While critical of many aspects of the workings of American democracy, he has not offered any suggestions for how it might be changed. Instead, like the Pied Piper of Hamelin, he attracts his followers and redirect them onto a devastating path, but only for his own personal gain and revenge. There is no debate, no compromise but hate, racism, fascism and provocation. He and his followers ignore any democratic responsibility.

Dwight D. Eisenhower made a significant comment on compromise and a long process of debate in US democratic process: "Without exhaustive debate, even heated debate, of ideas and programs, free government would weaken and wither. But if we allow ourselves to be persuaded that every individual or party that takes issue with our own convictions is necessarily wicked or treasonous then, indeed, we are approaching the end of freedom's road."

Undoubtedly, Trump's enthusiastic supporters and backers add a singular, energetic dimension to the Republican primary, one that ignores their national responsibility. Few political analysts and pundits expect that such a campaign can survive this general election.

However, now, such predictions have failed. Trump is winning, stunning his critics. There are many signs of an indication of the doom that is waiting to descend on the Republican Party itself before it does on the nation. This party, being thrown out by American liberals and peace lovers, is now getting desperate to win, and is resorting to a campaign as nakedly and deliberately fascistic as Trump is in its attempts to secure the presidency. This will prove to be a fatal strategy if the Republicans lose this election. Their next move will be to be even more fascistic to create chaos and use force to change the tide of the next election. Now everything is possible in the US political spectrum.

As Henry A. Wallace said in 1944, "The dangerous American fascist is the man who wants to do in the United States in an American way what Hitler did in Germany in a Prussian way. The American fascist would prefer not to use violence. His method is to poison the channels of public information. With a fascist the problem is never how best to present the truth to the public but how best to use the news to deceive the public into giving the fascist and his group more money or more power...

"Still another danger is represented by those who, paying lip service to democracy and the common welfare, in their insatiable greed for money and the power which money gives, do not hesitate surreptitiously to evade the laws designed to safeguard the public from monopolistic extortion...

"The American fascists are most easily recognized by their deliberate perversion of truth and fact. Their newspapers and propaganda carefully cultivate every fissure of disunity, every crack in the common front against fascism... They claim to be super-patriots, but they would destroy every liberty guaranteed by the Constitution. They demand free enterprise, but are the spokesmen for monopoly and vested interest. Their final objective toward which all their deceit is directed is to capture political power so that, using the power of the state and the power of the market simultaneously, they may keep the common man in eternal subjection."

Here Trump plays his deceitful game very well. Trump understands his position as an indirect fascist who never likes to be considered a fascist. This is why he has never called upon the shock troops of a paramilitary wing for support, and has always maintained a great and visible distance from the white nationalists and neo-Nazis who have become some of his most enthusiastic backers in this political campaign. He is never really one of them but uses them in his fascistic campaign.

"Trump", as Chip Bertlet says, "is a classic right-wing nativist populist demagogue: His ideology and rhetoric are much more comparable to the European populist radical right, akin to Jean-Marie Le Pen's National Front, the Danish People's Party or Vladimir Zhirinovsky's Liberal Democratic Party of Russia. All of them use the common radical right rhetoric of nativism, authoritarianism and populism."

Bertlet continues, "The leaders of organized political or social movements sometimes tell their followers that a specific group of "Others" is plotting to destroy civilized society. History tells us that if this message is repeated vividly enough, loudly enough, often enough, and long enough—it is only a matter of time before the bodies from the named scapegoated groups start to turn up."

Yes, Trump is plotting to destroy a civilized society through his fascism, but his fascism is malignant, metastasized in version, crazed in its insatiable lust for power, fueled by fear and hatred in the disguise of word-cannibalism, and fed by the red and fresh blood of its vulnerable and weak targets.

Aldous Huxley, an English writer, novelist, and philosopher, said, "By means of ever more effective methods of mind-manipulation, the democracies will change their nature; the quaint old forms—elections, parliaments, Supreme Courts and all the rest—will remain. The underlying substance will be a new kind of non-violent totalitarianism. All the traditional names, all the hallowed slogans will remain exactly what they were in the good old days. Democracy and freedom will be the theme of every broadcast and editorial. Meanwhile the ruling oligarchy and its highly trained elite of soldiers, policemen, thought-manufacturers and mind-manipulators will quietly run the show as they see fit."

Huxley's remark echoes when Trump is now running the show in this election campaign through his non-violent fascism. However, some political leaders have already called him a fascist. New Democratic Party Leader in Canada Tom Mulcair condemned Trump as a "fascist" and criticized his Prime Minister Justin Trudeau for not denouncing the fascist billionaire business mogul.

"Donald Trump is a fascist. Let's not kid ourselves, let's not beat around the bush," Mulcair said in a question-and-answer session after a speech to party staff recently.

Trump does not represent a para-military force yet. What he represents, instead, is the kind of savage and power politics common to the radical right, the demand for ideological and biological purity that are the very tenets of full-fledged fascism. What he is looking for in this election, other than wining it, is a silent and non-violent revolution advancing his fascist ideologies.

That does not, however, mean he is any less dangerous to American democracy, even to his own empire. Indeed, he may be more dangerous than an outright fascist, who would in reality be far less appealing and far less likely to succeed in the current political spectrum. What Trump is doing, by exploiting the elements of right-wing populism in the country, is making the large and growing body of proto-fascists in America larger and even more vicious. That is, he is creating the conditions that could easily lead to a genuine and potentially irrevocable outbreak of fascism, which will take a severe and devastating turn if he wins. Even some of the white populists and proto-fascists may not have any idea what a dangerous turn Trump might take to ruin their country if he wins.

Then this full-blown outbreak of fascism will be uncontrollable, dominating all of the US, controlling and punishing the media and corporations who didn't listen to him. This is one of the reasons why Trump is getting so much media attention and Ted Cruz is so careful while talking to Trump even in a debate.

It is by tiny drops of rising meanness and viciousness that how some Americans have lost their sense of humanity and democracy. The Nazis, at the end of their fight, had the inexorable ascension of cruel and dark inhumanity, but they didn't get that way in months. They got that way through year after year of attacking and demonizing, then regrouping and urging the elimination of those they thought to be their serious enemies.

And this is what has been happening to America, in particular, to the conservative movement and the Republican Party, for a very long time that really started back in the 1990s when Americans first experienced in the media the popular rise of eliminationist hate talk, used with thoughtless elation and great uniformity by an increasing number of sick right-wing pundits led by Rush Limbaugh.

Then these hate-talkers have subsequently marched across the bright stages at Fox News, which was considered the right place for them to catch nation-wide attention. Then this drive became dormant for a while. It surfaced again with the vice-presidential candidacy of Sarah Palin in 2008, followed immediately, in reaction to the election of Barack Obama for his second term in 2012. Then this reactionary sentiment among them gave the birth of the Tea Party, which is perhaps the single most significant manifestation of right-wing populism in America's history.

Mainstream conservatives built more and more ideological bridges with the right wing, reflected in the increasing adoption of far-right rhetoric within the sprawling mainstream. The elements of populism and authoritarianism became more and more imbedded in the mainstream-conservative political structure, particularly the deep, and often irrational hatred of the federal government.

And additionally, with this deep hatred rose nativism, authoritarianism and populism, the key features always visible in the mainstream ideologies and mass attitude in America.

A few years later, Trump paralleled himself with the manifestation of the Tea Party and enthusiastically got himself involved in 2011 with a comment: "I represent a lot of the ingredients of the Tea Party." And yes, he was correct, in particular, with his homage to the gurus of the hate-industry and their insatiable intention for making profits at the expense of everyone else.

Usually, white-nationalist websites often mock the Republicans as Zionist stooges and corporate puppets who opened the borders in order to keep wages low. However, on July 9th, 2015, VDARE, an opinion website to "push back the plans of pro-Amnesty and Immigration Surge by politicians, ethnic activists and corrupt Big Business," and hailed Trump as "the first figure with the financial, cultural, and economic resources to openly defy elite consensus. If he can mobilize Republicans behind him and make a credible run for the Presidency, he can create a whole new media environment for patriots to openly speak their mind without fear of losing their jobs." The interesting article was titled, "WE ARE ALL DONALD TRUMP NOW."

Then Trump "made an incredible surge among the Tea Party supporters," according to Patrick Murray, who runs polling for Monmouth University. Before Trump announced his candidacy, only twenty per cent of Tea Partiers had a favorable view of him; a month later, that figure had risen to fifty-six per cent.

Trump became the top choice among Tea Party voters, supplanting Senator Ted Cruz of Texas, and Governor Scott Walker of Wisconsin, both Tea Party stalwarts. According to a *Washington Post*/ABC News poll, the "broad majority" of Trump's supporters hailed from two groups: voters with no college degree, and voters who say that immigrants weaken America. By mid-August, Trump was even closing in on Hillary Clinton. CNN reported that, when voters were asked to choose between the two, Clinton was leading fifty-one per cent to forty-five.

One of the more popular "mainstream" figures among this right-wing populist bloc in the 1990s was Republican Ron Paul of Texas. And so, when he created something of a sensation with his campaign for the Republican nomination in 2008, it meant that these ideas and agendas started receiving widespread circulation among the mainstream right, and with it, an increasing number of conservatives who called themselves "libertarians", when what they really meant was "populists." It was done silently and, off course, without any political discourse.

But if Ron Paul opened the door for right-wing populism, he scarcely could have anticipated the overnight political star who would, in short order, come breezing through it: Sarah Palin. Her style is a somewhat different and sensational. She represents a more mainstream-friendly brand of right-wing populism, and as a result, it was embraced by a significantly greater portion of the American electorate.

Her populism emerged for national view shortly after John McCain announced her as his running mate. It was more than just the aggressive, McCarthyite attacks on Obama as a "radical" who "palled around with Muslim terrorists" and the paranoid bashing of "liberal elites." Most of all, there was the continuous suggestion that she and McCain represented "real Americans" and were all about standing up for "the people."

Populism, yes, but indisputably right-wing, too: socially and fiscally conservative, business-friendly, and hostile to progressive causes. The populist narrative was constant and current in Palin's speeches, particularly when she got the crowd chanting, "Drill, baby, drill!" in front of her illegitimate grandchild.

The almost dormant populism lashed up by Palin's candidacy became active and manifest as a national movement in short order with the rise of the Tea Party in 2009. Indeed, not only was the Tea Party overtly a right-wing populist movement, it soon became a major reason for the revival of the 1990s version of this populism, the "Patriot" militia movement. Many of these Tea Partiers are now the same Oath Keepers whose members widely support Trump's candidacy.

For many scholars, right-wing populist supporters are classified as part of the "radical right," while the term "extreme right" is reserved for insurgent, actively violent groups seeking to overturn the constitutional order.

Of course, most of these extremists are only one step removed, ideologically speaking, from the neo-Nazism and other white supremacists of the racist right, and both of those segments of the right lean heavily on nativist and authoritarian rhetoric, having Trump as their guru.

And there really is no other good word for Trump's rhetoric, and the behavior of many of his followers, than "fascistic." So it is only natural that Trump's right-wing populism has already turned into fascism even though he doesn't yet have armed supporters marching on the streets. Did Hitler before the Reichstag? No, not until he got the power in Reichstag. Every fascist is a right-wing populist and their political journey is deeply rooted in populism.

All of this underscores the central fact: Donald Trump may not be a fascist, but his vicious brand of right-wing populism is not just empowering the latent fascist elements in America, he is leading a whole nation, as the Pied Piper of Hamelin did, of followers merrily down a path that leads directly to fascism. And this is not going to stop soon, even if Trump loses.

The rise of Trump has shown the world the disturbing elements in American society and the failure of the US political system to protect all of its citizens. But Trump has radicalized these features using the fear, anti-intellectualism and ignorance of the supporters who believe, in a larger scale, in these ideologies.

Scary is his that followers are serious. When Trump made a comment about "roughing up" Black Lives Matter protesters, two nights later, a trio of white supremacists in Minneapolis invaded a Black Lives Matter protest and shot five people, in a heinous act that had been carefully planned and networked through the Internet. It shows the might of the proto-para-military of Trump.

Trump has achieved this kind of high level of influence and publicity through his business branding, where he has gained immense power and momentum. So, he is able to simply demonize a target with rhetoric suggestive of violence, and his supporters will act out that very suggestion. It is scary for every liberal. It is only a step away from the fascist leader who calls out his paramilitary thugs to engage in violence. Trump is trying to be a fascist demigod to win the votes of Southern states, right-wing white populist votes, KKKs votes, racist fringes' votes. This is how he plans to defeat Ted Cruz.

What is most troubling, though, is the momentum that Trump's candidacy has given that wave. He may not himself lack any real ideological stability, but he has lain the groundwork for a fascist outpouring that could someday be ridden to power by a similarly charismatic successor who is himself more in the mold of an ideological fascist, maybe in a nonviolent way. And it doesn't take a very long look down the roll of 2016 Republican candidates to find a candidate who might fit that mold.

Trump may not be a Nazi, but he is empowering existing elements of Nazism in American society; even more dangerously, his Tea Party brand of right-wing populism is helping them grow their ranks, along with their potential to recruit large numbers. Not only that, he is making all this thuggery and ugliness seem normal. And that is a serious problem.

It is mentionable here that Nazism is a version of fascism, in the same way Trumpism can be an American version of fascism.

At last, there are four components in Trump's presidential campaign that invoke parallels to Nazism.

1. Trump's intense cult-like personality, which, for Trump supporters, is particularly driven by his business branding, by his reputation as a successful businessman who can "fix things," "make a great deal," "I can do better," and by his willingness to shamelessly defy the norms of political correctness of modern American democracy.

Trump uses salvos of brazen racist demagoguery. He declares offensively that undocumented Mexican immigrants are largely criminals and rapists, and in his recent proposal he said Muslims should carry ID cards identifying their religion. He means segregation in USA, this time the way the Jewish were segregated in Hitler's Germany.

2. There are the undertones of violence in his provocative and hate speeches, both inspired by his rhetoric (e.g., the two Bostonians who savagely assaulted a homeless Hispanic man and urinated on his face while invoking Trump's name) and directly advocated by Trump himself (e.g., his open agreement with supporters at a Trump rally in Birmingham, Alabama, who pushed down, kicked, and punched a black protester).

3. Not only this, another example of fascism is that Trump is notorious for being sexist, and sexism is a tenet of fascism. Fascist societies are completely male-dominated. Trump is a sexist like most of fascist leaders in German history.

Trump attacks Carly Fiorina, his Republican rival, for her looks: "Look at that face!" he said on TV. "Would anyone vote for that? Can you imagine that, the face of our next president?!" And he did it so unapologetically, without any remorse, because of his fascist nature.

The day after his first ever appearance in a national televised Republican debate, Trump attacked Megyn Kelly, the Fox channel moderator as having "blood coming out of wherever," insinuating that she was menstruating during the performance.

Women? He once told *Esquire*, "You know, it doesn't really matter what [the media] write as long as you've got a young and beautiful piece of ass."

Nasty and personal fights, which are the essential elements to create suspense and excitement in reality programs, have become almost predictable traits of Trump's political campaign as well.

Trump's mini-Trumps even go further. A group of Donald Trump supporters were being hosted in a TV show in USA. The anchor was Samantha Bee. An excerpt from that talk show:

"I think you're kind of a trickle-down media whore," one Trump supporter told Samantha Bee in a conversation during the talk show.

"So in the big bukkake of media," Bee replied, "I'm the one at the bottom of the fuck pile?"

"I think that's an accurate assessment," quoted the Trump supporter.

Trump has now somewhat outgrown in the right-wing populist periphery, even that once skeptical relationship he had with the right-wing populists, and has become an equal opportunity hater, turning his nativist, misogynist rage on general allies who sometimes disagree with him, even his opponent Republican candidate like Ted Cruz.

A collection of ultra-nationalist, white supremacist, right-wing racist American states, which consider themselves to have been betrayed by politicians, are now enticed by

Trump's insurgency. And his insurgency got stronger when officially Sarah Palin endorsed him in this election of 2016.

But this is an ominous sign for fair US democracy. The world has seen during 1930s in Europe, in every country, that this type of movement was committed to destroying their own country's independence and sovereignty by aiding Hitler to conquer it. What could explain Trump's popularity in a country that made fascism a dirty word following the fall of Hitler and Mussolini?

Fascism has been thoughtfully mapping out the descent of a civilized people—first the Italians, then the Germans—now the mighty USA. Protecting American democracy against this growing fascism serves as a proof of American power and responsibility. Also, his fascism throws a dark shadow on his empire. Is it going to survive? When Trump supporters and swing voters are told that the Republican candidate is a fascist or latter-day Hitler, it is easy for them to dismiss those concerns as partisan hyperbole, if for no other reason that they can't really conceive of this idea. After all, America has never elected an outright Nazi to the presidency, so that particular threat seems more hypothetical than actual. Actually, many Americans probably welcome the idea now. Not so when talking about patterns of institutional discrimination that, though often overlooked by the media, were demonstrably all-too-real chapters of American history.

Trump's political power, as well as the power of the right-wing reactionaries who will follow in his footsteps, comes from his ability to create a cult of personality for himself while effectively capitalizing on America's latent racism, sexism, and other forms of prejudice. Just because these things don't make him a neo-Nazi doesn't mean they wouldn't be devastating for America.

That's why Americans must resist the urge to characterize Trump's racial demagoguery, cult of personality, and authoritarian policy proposals as fascist or in any other way Hitleresque. By doing this, they deny and potentially empower the brutality, oppression, and violence that has marked so much of America's political history. Trump is certainly pandering to the American nation's worst instincts, but the sentiments into which he has tapped successfully with serious media attention have been with this country for a long, long time, and have left deep marks. Trump, after many years, has just opened the dark and racist side of American history. The long-buried stinks have surfaced again, which is a net loss and shame for sensitive and conscientious Americans.

When some American pundits imply that the sinister Trump phenomenon represents something new on the American scene, they ignore the ugliest parts of US political history, and in the process make it more likely that those mistakes will be repeated this time as well, by Donald Trump. A question arises about the effectiveness of the evolution process in US politics and how much does the US gain from it.

Is Trump Getting His Clues From Hitler?

Donald Trump is an apparent fan of Adolf Hitler's speeches. Quite a few of his addresses reflects Hitler's tone, strategy and posture. Some say, Donald is a new American Hitler in the making of new generation of Hitler's passionate followers on the soil of America.

It is stunning but not entirely surprising and unexpected revelation that comes from his ex-wife Ivana Trump, who told *Vanity Fair* in a 1990 interview that "from time to time her husband reads a book of Hitler's collected speeches, *My New Order*, which he keeps in a cabinet by his bed." The magazine said Trump confirmed he got it from a film industry friend, Marty Davis. "I thought he would find it interesting," Davis said. "I am his friend, but I'm not Jewish," he added.

My New Order by Adolf Hitler is a famous book, published after Hitler's two-volume *Mein Kampf* (*My Struggle*). [Literally, my camp (or party).] *My New Order* was published in 1925 and 1926, before the Nazi rise to national power, and World War II. It is not just a collection of excerpts from speeches Hitler made between 1918 and 1941; it is profusely indexed and filled with meticulous detail about the speeches' impact on the media and political establishment in Germany and right across Europe.

Ivana's statement to *Vanity Fair* supports the rest of the magazine's profile of a real estate tycoon who loved to live in the public eye and manipulate media coverage with his clear strategy. Trump, after confirming he had the book, later told the reporter, "If I had these speeches, and I am not saying that I do, I would never read them."

It is clear now that Trump's rise is similar to the populist movement of Germany. Frightened and confused by economic weakness, Islamophobia and immigration pressure, US right-wing voters are willing to toss out the political incumbents and let the billionaire try to implement the ideas in his provocative speeches. The well-written, rehearsed, and polished speeches of the seasoned politicians are not simply managing voters' expectations of authenticity.

On the other hand, Trump voters think Trump says what he honestly believes, which resonate with their beliefs. They see him as not caring about the consequences of his style and language. Some political pundits think, Donald Trump doesn't have a deep hunger to be president, but instead is expanding and strengthening his business branding. This gives him great rhetorical freedom. "Trump may sound absurd to some, but no one doubts he believes what he says." In the same way, fascists believe what they are doing.

Seemingly, Trump has absorbed much of the content in *My New Order* about how Hitler says propaganda works, how he structures and designs his speaking style, and how Hitler targeted the lowest-common denominator of German political electorate as his intended audience. This is clearly noticeable in the way he speaks, argues, rages and responds to the media and his own audience.

Trump's propaganda has worked for him perfectly. Once he falsely claimed that he had seen "thousands and thousands" of Muslims in Jersey City watching and cheering as the World Trade Center towers came down on 9/11. Later, it was found out that there was no base for his such claim. It was false propaganda against American Muslims.

The *New York Times* took a great initiative to analyze Trump's personality. They analyzed 95,000 words from five months of Trump's political speeches and concluded that Trump shares a style with the 20th century's biggest demagogues.

Trump's speeches contain simplistic racist attacks with provocation and hatred. He demeaned his president, who was visiting Ethiopia. He did it because he was offended by the presence of a black man in the White House. He demeans and insults his competitors for the 2016 Republican presidential nomination. He slates Democrats' political "correctness" as weak and absurd.

He mocks women and disabled people. He has been hateful to Blacks and The Native Americans. He threatens to obliterate the enemies he names in his political campaign. He doesn't care about numbers, facts or inconsistencies, and preys on his followers' fears and prejudices.

All of these tactics, from the repetitive style of his speeches, to believing whatever he says is true, to his excessive and unrivaled view of his leadership, are modeled on Hitler in his book *My New Order*, according to a psychological profile of the book in the September 2013 issue of the scholarly journal, *Psychiatric Quarterly*. "The elements of a delusional system are there," it states. "This is not simply to say that the man is mad and so has plunged the world into chaos; but it is to say that there is overwhelming evidence in 19 years of his speeches that Hitler himself firmly believes many of his most absurd declarations, including some, which are contradictory."

Obama's low ratings not only indicate voters' resentment of Washington's policies on domestic and international issues, but also the resentment of the young generation of democracy itself, which is not working. They think democracy is a clear trade-bait. It doesn't ensure Washington's promises and effectiveness in fulfilling their commitments even though a large number of Americans believe Obama's management of the US economy has been stunningly successful.

These young voters, right-wing populists and KKK members find an alternative in fascism, which teaches violence in an ordered and civilized society. Trump and his followers fit into this mould.

Whether he uses *My New Order* as a textbook, Trump's way of leading these disgruntled people is stunningly similar to Hitler's writings about how propaganda works. In addition to the collection of speeches and their impact, *Mein Kampf* has a chapter on the hows and whys of political propaganda. Look at these six excerpts from Ralph Manheim's 1943 translation that have been put into a "Teachers Guide To The Holocaust," produced by the University of South Florida. Hitler wrote:

1. "The function of propaganda does not lie in the scientific training of the individual, but in calling the masses' attention to certain facts, processes, necessities, etc., whose significance is thus for the first time placed within their field of vision.

2. "All propaganda must be popular and its intellectual level must be adjusted to the most limited intelligence among those it is addressed to. Consequently, the greater the mass it is intended to reach, the lower its purely intellectual level will have to be.

3. "The more modest its intellectual ballast, the more exclusively it takes into consideration the emotions of the masses, the more effective it will be. And this is the best proof of the soundness or unsoundness of a propaganda campaign, and not success pleasing a few scholars or young aesthetes.

4. "Once understood how necessary it is for propaganda to be adjusted to the broad mass, the following rule results: It is a mistake to make propaganda many-sided, like scientific instruction, for instance.

5. "In consequence of these facts, all effective propaganda must be limited to a very few points and must harp on these in slogans until the last member of the public understands what you want him to understand by your slogan.

6. "The function of propaganda is, for example, not to weigh and ponder the rights of different people, but exclusively to emphasize the one right which it has set out to argue for. Its task is not to make an objective study of the truth...its task is to serve our own right, always and unflinchingly."

Trump is following Hitler in this election campaign, no doubt about it. He is unapologetic, remorseless in his provocative and hateful speeches, which are very wrong in a democratic environment, but he does not care because of his fascistic movement and agenda.

Following Trump's call for a ban on all Muslim immigrants, newspapers and digital media outlets around the world responded with tired Nazi comparisons. In particular, the *Philadelphia Daily News* and the *Times of Israel* paired their stories with images depicting Trump giving what looks like infamous Nazi salute.

The *Times of Israel*'s image selection was especially noticeable for two reasons, the first being that it was taken from Trump's speech at the Republican Jewish Coalition meeting. The New York real estate tycoon, standing before the crowd of conservative Jewish voters, is seen giving what looks an awful lot like Adolf Hitler's trademark stance.

The *Philadelphia Daily News*'s cover page directly compared Trump to Adolf Hitler, using a photo of the Republican presidential front-runner with his arm raised to look like a Nazi salute. The front-page headline was "A New Führer" - a pun to compare Trump to the German Führer.

But the Americans are not miserable enough to elect Donald Trump as their president while the misery index is deteriorating. Are they?

However, any miracle in even a harsh realistic society can negatively change the fate and light of American Democracy and some will simply say "good-bye." Even if Trump loses, and the right candidate wins the presidency, the campaign trail of Donald Trump will remain a shame for American Democracy and a nightmare for targeted and humiliated races and religions.

It is surprising to see that despite the continuity of changes in innovation, technology and lifestyles, religions prosper in America, because humanity needs to reduce its uncertainty in this universe.

But it is also clear the strength of the mighty US constitution can't protect its citizens, because of colors and religions, and the weak part of it is exposed by Donald Trump. Nothing is intangible, nothing to be so much proud of, it is all dark when the darkness of other side of human life comes out with all its sharp edges. This darkness can live up to its limit only either in a dark cave or in a beaconing and well-branded fantasy house.

Europe was a dark continent in the 20th century. Now North America may be a dark continent soon if Trump wins, if his followers keep on growing in numbers and in their fascist agenda. Hitler made mistakes, so did Trump. What will be the consequences of Trump's mistakes? Will he understand that instead of a real estate legend, he has become a demagogue?

Trump's Freedom And Liberty

The "political correctness," which in real term does not exist anymore in this time of the election year of 2016, used to be once distinctive American pride: democracy, freedom and humanity.

However, Donald's defense of liberty, freedom and security appears designed to persuade people in power rather than the common people.

For decades, all American media, regardless of persuasion, have covered Trump's unapologetic vulgarity, his willingness to say absolutely anything. Thus he has gradually built up a unique Freedom of the Press for himself, for his branding. He began to build his own school of freedom and liberty in the land of freedom and liberty for all.

He is a pure child of the USA, a big apple on Apple Street. He knows the tactful and smooth art of catching out his opponents' mistakes, failures and incompetence. He knows genuinely when and how to strike at them, and how hard. He becomes terribly emotional, with vicious, threatening expressions. His quotes statements are often rude, aggressive, provoking where humanity does not persist but he keeps winning primaries after primaries.

Recently, through his incendiary comments, Donald Trump has been accepted by a new American brand of democracy - without the very notions of equality and freedom for all, where politics has become some sort of entertainment, nurturing of power and arrogance, and flirting with humble followers. This politicization of entertainment got tremendous momentum during the first presidential election of Barack Obama, and the circus continues with sensationalism for all Americans, and the world! It is also amusing.

The logic that uses the profit motive in politics and entertainment to justify crimes against humanity is beyond being immoral. Somehow, the notion of healthy competition in US presidential elections has morphed into a rapidly metastasizing strain of hate and provocative crime, showing that equality is not for all in America, at least not for the Muslims, Hispanics and the Blacks.

Donald has violated the loftiest ideals of America— freedom and equality that so many Americans were proud of. Trump's arrival is the escape of equality and freedom, and US democracy languishes. Americans have struggled for a long time to achieve their coveted equality and freedom, but their achievement was never complete, and Trump has shown it will never be. Equality is one of the greatest hoaxes in American political culture.

Donald Trump's campaign has been destroying, mocking or abusing equality of opportunity, freedom of speech, individual liberty. He has been a consistent opponent of marriage equality. Probably, even he believes in the empirical reality that human beings are either male or female. More recently he expressed support for the so-called First Amendment Defense Act (FADA), which would expose LGBT people to more discrimination. Trump said he would

"Strongly Consider" appointing judges to overturn the same-sex marriage decision, which was the result of a long struggle.

The background of this struggle is very deep and long-standing. As Alexis de Tocqueville noted, Americans venerate both liberty and equality. America's entire history involves this tension between preserving freedom and promoting equality.

An inconsistency is that Americans also believe that "success in life" is determined by individual effort and not by outside forces. Trump has negated this in some statements discussing the fact that many Anglo-Saxon Americans are jobless, with declining wealth. They must regroup and rebuild crippled America. Here, he defies the very notion of capitalism: of individual effort resulting in gaining wealth. Instead, he is providing an outside force, regrouping and empowering Anglo-Saxons.

On the other hand, Trump defies freedom, the freedom of Muslims, Blacks, Hispanics, and disabled people. And the freedom of these groups will be compromised greatly if he becomes the first fascist President in US history. Trump, dominated by extreme right-wing populists, has no design to include all in his concept of freedom and liberty. This means that equality and freedom will evaporate from America.

Trump's school of equality and freedom is based on duality and hypocrisy.

But white-populist, right-wing Americans love it, leading to a total degeneration in politics and its culture. Where to go now to learn democracy and equality? Which well-branded University in the USA can be used to study healthy concurrent political thoughts in the USA?

Trump hurt John McCain, the former Republican presidential candidate, damaged his fame and the respect for war veterans. Thus he had made young US generations to question Military service. But the problem is not only Trump here, but the media outlets who love to broadcast his heinous comment on the respected war veteran, John McCain. And most of the Republicans love for his comment proves time has changed significantly putting an end of an old and fundamental values. It is entertaining flirting with Trump. After all, he has money, so much of it. And above all, he has his own school of freedom and liberty. He can do and say whatever he likes.

The candidate selection process involves greed, gruesome fighting, backstabbing during the presidential elections, but the current round has exceeded all precedents. Why has US society degenerated so much? And what poison we can expect, should Trump become the President of the USA—the most powerful man in the most powerful nation? Where is the collective social conscience of the USA? Or is the US completely morally broke now? Then, for how long and by what right can a broken country dictate to the world without the kinds of destructive actions we have seen in the Middle East?

If Trump becomes President, will he ignore the Constitution, having his own brand of freedom and liberty?

Will there be a nuclear war with either Iran or North Korea? Will there be new invasions on foreign lands, further depleting the US economy? This may happen, because this man does not care for human lives, human civilization and values. Personal greed is above all things, winning is above all things—the value system of his fascistic political philosophy.

His school of political thought is not the classic one that made the US strong and proud since even before its foundation was laid. His school is full of racism, populism, fascism, demagoguery, provocation and flirting with the people of lowest denominator of the US political electorate. His school is a school of abomination and anti-democracy, except, that proud history that includes treachery, betrayal and genocide against Native Americans, slavery of the Irish and Africans, exploitation of workers, the consumer lifestyle that is destroying the environment.

Will Americans put God and their country at the forefront and vote for a normal and decent Presidential candidate who will better represent the country and make every American proud again regardless of their color, gender, race and religion? Will Americans lead the world with the grandeur of democracy, and show decency, and the memorable tradition of democracy in this election? Will Americans elect someone who will be a leader, a thinker to lead the country to another stage where the world will watch and follow the USA for its betterment? Will Americans elect someone who will destroy the peace-destroyers and establish democracy, peace and world prosperity? Will Americans elect someone who will have a sense of shame for deliberately and repeatedly lying?

We will see the true spirit of the Americans in November 2016.

If Trump Wins:

It is a political fantasy to think Trump as an elected president, some political analysts and pundits think. Despite this thought and vision, still Trump has a chance to win. After all, money speaks in this multi-billion-dollar election campaign. If Donald Trump wins the presidency, there will be a long flow of changes at domestic and international level, which will be decisive and, in some situations, confrontational.

If he doesn't win:
1. The world will sigh in relief
2. It will take time for the Republicans to clean up their house
3. Trump's credibility will fade

4. His own world will be crippled
5. His empire may come close to failure
6. His branding may become ineffective around the globe
7. Fascist, nativist and populist elements will remain in US society and will be waiting for another Donald Trump to become a Yankee Hitler.
8. Some may unnecessarily think to ban the Republican Party but it can't happen because US democracy has only two legs.

Trump may do a few things quickly if he does win:

1. Restrictions on Muslim visits and migration to the USA.

2. There will be a large, high wall along the long Mexican-American Border. The undocumented Mexican immigrant issue will be solved, until the Mexicans find another way to enter US. And he will cut off cash to Mexico to cover the expense of the wall.

3. Trump will change his political stance if he becomes President of USA. He may distance himself from right-wing fringes, which will put him in some sort of confrontational position with them

4. He will dim American democracy. American culture, politics and administration will be dominated by extreme right-wing populists.

This means that equality and freedom will evaporate from America.

5. His business empire will continue to increase.

If Donald is the President, America will be at stake, and the Constitution may go through another amendment to make the life of some minorities a hell. It will be easier for him as Congress has Republican majority and it will remain as it is for a while. Donald Trump's policies and comments are terrifying for some races in the USA. Multiculturalism doesn't remain, and integration among all races is not possible when a person like Trump smashes all the good things in a multicultural mosaic built over decades. Even if Trump is defeated in the Presidential run, his roots will remain deep in US society, a cause of concern for racial harmony.

But he has already made comments on some other political and immigration issues:

First, on the deportation issue: When asked how he would implement it, he has said that he would have a "deportation force" to find, detain and repatriate suspected undocumented immigrants and their children, some of whom are Americans.

When quizzed in the debates he had this to say to John Kasich's assertion that deporting all these millions of people is not a serious proposal: "All I can say is, you're lucky in Ohio that you struck oil. That's for one thing. Let me just tell you that Dwight Eisenhower, good president, great president. People liked him. Moved 1.5 million illegal immigrants out of this country. Moved them just beyond the border. They came back. Moved them again beyond the border. They came back. Didn't like it. Moved them way south. They never came back."

He, of course, plans to build a wall so high on the borders that no Mexicans can climb over it. But that comment was not a joke. He was talking about the infamous Operation

Wetback of that time. And those Mexican immigrants never came back because they had been left in the middle of the desert without water and died.

Second, he has openly said he would commit war crimes and explicitly target the families of suspected ISIS terrorists: "We're fighting a very politically correct war. And the other thing with the terrorists—you have to take out their families. When you get these terrorists, you have to take out their families! They care about their lives, don't kid yourselves. They say they don't care about their lives. But you have to take out their families."

Third, on the domestic front, Trump has made it very, very clear that in addition to his "deportation force," he believes the country needs to allow much more autonomy to police agencies: "We're going to get, you know, the gang members in Baltimore and in Chicago and these are some tough dudes. They're going to be out so fast. One of the first thing I'm going to do is get rid of those gang members. We're going to be - know, you look at what's going on with Baltimore, you look at what's going on in Chicago and Ferguson and St. Louis the other night. We are going to get rid of those gang members so fast your head will spin.

You know, we can be very tough. I just met your cops outside. Those police are tough cookies. Those guys—we need law and order. We need law and order. I mean, they allowed— in one night, that first night in Baltimore—they allowed that city to be destroyed. And they set it back 35 years. One night. Because the police were not allowed to protect people. They weren't allowed to protect people."

It is notable here that under fascist regimes, the police or local para-militaries are given almost boundless power to enforce laws. The people are so paranoid with patriotism cum fascism that they are often willing to overlook police abuses, and even forego civil liberties in the name of patriotism. There is often a national police force with virtually unlimited power in fascist nations.

He insists citizens should spy on each other and report activities to the authorities. And he made a solemn pledge to police everywhere: "One of the first things I'd do in terms of executive order, if I win, will be to sign a strong, strong statement that would go out to the country, out to the world: anybody killing a police man, a police woman, a police officer, anybody killing a police officer, the death penalty is going to happen."

Fourth, considering the summary execution farce he does on the campaign trail every day when he talks about Bowe Bergdahl, it is fair to assume he has some ideas about how that might be handled. And he enthusiastically endorsed torture that he will implement if he wins. And not just for interrogation purposes but as a punitive measure: "Would I approve waterboarding? You bet your ass I would—in a heartbeat," Trump said to loud cheers during a rally at a convention center that attracted thousands. "And I would approve more than that. Don't kid yourself, folks. It works, okay? It works. Only a stupid person would say it doesn't work."

Trump said, such techniques are needed to confront terrorists who "chop off our young people's heads" and "build these iron cages, and they'll put 20 people in them and they drop them in the ocean for 15 minutes and pull them up 15 minutes later."

"It works," Trump has said over and over again. "Believe me, it works. And you know what? If it doesn't work, they deserve it anyway, for what they're doing. It works."

When asked what he would do with the families of suspected terrorists, he was unclear, but when you consider his other commentary, the implication is clear: "I would certainly go after the wives who absolutely knew it was happening, and

I guess your definition of what I'd do, I'm going to leave that to your imagination."

Imagination! He has a serious fantasy about the wives of the 9/11 hijackers, imagining that those women had foreknowledge of the attacks, and tuned in on TV with their children to watch their daddies fly into the World Trade Center in Manhattan. Except for the fact that these hijackers weren't married and had no kids, otherwise it would be an interesting tale. However, Trump's supporters rejoiced in what he said, never questioned his claims. The Trumpian propaganda continues to fool humble and gullible followers. Smart Trump realizes that these paranoid and hateful followers want to hear what they want to hear, not what the truth is.

He had also vividly shown his colors with his daily attacks against Bowe Bergdahl, whom he called a "dirty, rotten, traitor" who would have been summarily executed back in the day "when we were strong." He promised to make American military so strong their heads would spin and he declared himself a big second amendment person. He promised to "renegotiate deals" with every country in the world to get a better result for America, although he was vague about exactly what that meant beyond complaining about all the foreign cars he allegedly sees coming off of ships in American ports.

In his book *The America We Deserve,* Trump stated, "I use language to speak my mind. Being blunt hasn't hurt me so far. I've lived my life as I choose and said what I wanted to say." That means, should he become President, he plans to implement what he has said in this campaign trail and will say in the future. This sounds scary.

The fate of any country is largely a function of that country's top leadership. The United States is no exception to this rule. While Trump leads in the polls for the Republican Party candidacy, it seems only appropriate that the Americans understand and think about the type of leader Donald Trump would be for the United States. As such, Trump's popularity in the polls also serves as an indicator of the current American culture.

Trump is in serious contention to win the Republican presidential nomination. His triumph in a general election is unlikely, but it is far from impossible. He is a man who may soon be making decisions about war and peace, who will have the codes of the nuclear box, who will decide which regulations are enforced and which are lifted, who will be responsible for nominating Supreme Court justices and representing America in the community of nations. This is not political entertainment for his voters. This is real politics, the real world where he needs to be decent, reasonable, wise and diplomatic to win American's interest. At this moment, he is not close to that. Rather, he is close to being a fascist, who will only use power, propaganda and torture.

Behind Trump's success is an unerring instinct for harnessing anger, resentment, and fear. His view of the economy is entirely nothing—only for Americans should win, others must lose. "We're going to make America great again," he said in his New Hampshire victory speech, "but we're going to do it the old-fashioned way. We're going to beat China, Japan, beat Mexico at trade. We're going to beat all of these countries that are taking so much of our money away from us on a daily basis. It's not going to happen anymore."

Trump answers America's rage with more rage. As the journalist Molly Ball observed, "All the other candidates say 'Americans are angry, and I understand.' Trump says, 'I'M angry.'" Trump doesn't offer solutions, but rather, he offers villains. His message isn't so much that he'll help the Americans as he'll hurt them.

Another of Trump's distinctive gift is the one that gets less attention but is perhaps more important—his complete lack of shame. Maybe this gift was inherited from his grandfather. It is easy to underestimate how important shame is in American politics. But shame can't restrain the politicians who find success through demagoguery. Most people feel shame when they're exposed as liars. But when they are seen as informed but not caring, then their behavior is thought cruel. Then the respected figures in their party condemn their actions, when experts dismiss their proposals, then they are mocked and protested, their political campaign is despised, and their career ends. They possibly get impeached somewhere and of course, there is an outcry in all sorts of media. Their voters run away.

But American society has changed significantly, because Trump doesn't. He has the reality television star's ability to operate entirely without shame, and that permits him to operate entirely without restraint in changing American society. It is the single scariest characteristic of his personality. It is the one that allows him to go where others won't, to say what others can't, to do what others won't.

Significantly, his instincts are an improvement on the Republican field, because he seems more dovish than neoconservatives in the GOP itself. And his instincts are less dismissive of the social safety net than libertarians like Rand Paul. But those candidates are checked by institutions that hold no sway over Trump. His temperament is so immature, his political base so unique, his reactions so strange, that what he would do or what he wouldn't do if he wins is unpredictable.

If he becomes president, he will disappoint most of the struggling working-class whites, who have suffered keenly from the collapse of the industrial economy. And a large part of the white populist movement falls in this working class. Nevertheless, a lot of them are left behind in the current economic recovery from the economic meltdown of the Bush era. Poorly educated white males are left behind, and the country is not better for them, and there are enough of those people to make a huge difference. They can make a powerful movement and they are ready for it because they know well they are not able to upgrade their skills to fit in this information era. They want a return to the old manufacturing jobs they can happily do.

As Trump has promised already, if he wins, he will bring back those jobs from China and other countries, but deliberately he fell short of the dilemma of pricing. A dozen screws made in China costing a buck or two will cost six dollars or more if it is made in the USA. And even bringing those jobs back to the US is very time consuming.

If Trump wins the US Presidency, there may be some possible changes in the domestic and international spectrum with a long-lasting impact:

a. More wars

Donald Trump will have a very hawkish stance in his foreign policy if he is elected as the President of the USA.

His vision for US foreign policy is pretty straight-forward: he will make America great again, and the rest of the world just needs to deal with it.

The candidate explained why the central theme of his campaign is resonating with voters during a recent interview with David Rennie, Washington bureau chief for *The Economist*.

"It's a concept of greatness for this country. They are tired of being ripped off by every single country that does business with us. Whether it's China, Japan, Mexico, Vietnam, [or] ... Japan," Trump said.

In Trump's view, the people running Washington right now are all talk and no action. Whether it's about confronting ISIS, signing international trade agreements or taking care of American veterans, the surprise frontrunner in the Republican primary race said the political elites currently running the country are "grossly incompetent."

"I actually think this election is going to be about competence. I'm a very competent person," Trump told Rennie.

At its core, Rennie says Trump's foreign policy is characterized by old-fashioned isolationism.

Beyond the old trope of political hawks versus doves, Rennie says, "What [Trump's] showing is that there's another very ancient tradition in America, which is the desire to be such a strong and powerful country that the rest of world certainly does not challenge you."

Trump likes to say, "I'm the most militaristic person."

But Rennie adds that, "he doesn't actually ever want to use [the military]."

Rennie asked Trump what he would do about the Chinese creating new military bases in disputed parts of the South China Sea, for instance. Trump answered, "It's a hostile move. And I would be talking to them very seriously about it. However, it is very far away, and we have a lot of problems, OK? And they're already built."

There would be exceptions, however, for US foreign policy under the leadership of President Trump. He told *The Economist* that while he was on record opposing the American-led invasion of Iraq in 2003, he would not hesitate to deploy US troops to seize the oil fields in Iraq and Syria.

"The lesson that [Trump has] drawn from the last 10 years is [that] Americans are sick and tired of trying to tidy up the rest of the world. And they just want the rest of the world to be a bit more frightened of America and mind its manners," Rennie says.

Trump said the only nation-building effort he is interested in is right here in the United States of America.

"We're spending all of our money nation-building in other places and they don't even want us, OK?" Trump said to Rennie in a 42-minute phone interview.

Trump said he would expect more from US allies as commander-in-chief of the US. He would make better deals with them. They would have to accept much greater responsibility for their own national security problems if he became president.

Trump sent a warning to the allies instead of diplomacy and negotiation. This is a poor and risky judgment, which cannot be categorized either in diplomacy or international relations.

Trump is a successful businessman, where he showed leadership. Predicting leadership behavior on the basis of past leadership behavior is smart, but not foolproof. But at a minimum, Trump's adherence to key habits of hiring spectacularly unsuccessful executives should be a warning sign, it does not, will not make him a successful president. Instead it will attract ridicule.

Does this mean that a President Trump will necessarily fall prey to the same weaknesses that have brought down previously successful leaders like Ken Lay of Enron, Dennis Kozlowski of Tyco, and Martin Winterkorn of Volkswagen? This a big-time risk. Does it warrant a close attention from all conscientious Americans? Yes, it does.

As for China, Trump said he would play hardball with Beijing on trade. He accused China of devaluing its currency and said he would hit the Chinese with import tariffs of up to 12 percent.

"They're going to stop playing games with us. Look, they have taken our jobs, they have taken our money, and on top of that they have loaned the money to us and we actually pay them interest now on money. We owe China and Japan each $1.4 trillion," Trump said.

The editors at *The Economist* looked at the overall implications of Trump's policy ideas and were less than impressed.

"Americans are waking up to the possibility that a man whose hobby is naming things after himself might—conceivably—be the nominee of the party of Lincoln and Reagan. It is worth spelling out why that would be a terrible thing," the editors wrote in the latest issue of the magazine.

"From an economics point-of-view, we think that if he did one-tenth of what he's planning, he would trigger a global trade war, which would cause a kind of global recession and cost lots of jobs," Rennie says.

Trump would start his deportations, and things would be violent. Migrants would get rounded up. Liberals would start protecting migrants. Confrontations and fights will ensure. Militias would take it upon themselves to do their own deportations.

This will get ugly and people will die.

Pomposity and fear-mongering may get him free air time in his campaign, but it also stirs up the most volatile faction of your party. Once you go down the road, you can't control them. They'll feel empowered and they'll take your rhetoric seriously. It will start an ugly race war. Bad will be worse.

b. More problems with US finances

Trump has already problems with Wall Street, having made negative comments about them. Will the US recover as it almost did under Obama and Biden?

However, in the NYSE and S&P, the shares of specific industry will go up because of Trump's connection with a certain part of the Wall Street. The increasing economic vulnerability and financial collapse will cause:

i. Segregation and discontent in social context
ii. Insurgency by right wing, white populist elements
iii. Racial tensions and sporadic violence

iv. A record number of US people will become homeless
v. A sudden rise in the prostitution industry, especially by single mothers having no other sources of support as it happened in 2008.

c. A turbulence in international relations

If Trump becomes the President of the USA, there may be a rise of alternative international leadership: individual countries or alliances.

i. Individual leadership: To fill the gap, the single leaderships like UK, Germany and China, even Russia can come forward to lead the world and resolve the world problems like ISIS, terrorism, climate changes, poverty and the Palestinian issues. To maintain the balance of power, Trump may lean towards more military power instead of leadership and diplomacy which may put tremendous burden on US economy. And this weakness will encourage other nations to become new power brokers in the world stage.

ii. Unified leadership: The EU or a group of other emerging countries like China, India and Brazil can be united to make up the hole created by the US leadership means any military or diplomatic responses to security crises - both preventative efforts and beyond them – have to come from a wider group of nations and organizations than before. If it happens, then this will be a strategic loss for the US in security and global governance. And all these will happen because of Trump's lack of understanding world politics and international relations and because of his arrogance, ignorance and raw power.

Trump has failed to give the future role and the answer of how to make more effective international institutions, and American presidential politics and the foreign and security issues implications for America's future global role. He is not even aware of the cost to America of the wrong choices made by him.

America is already paying a cost for the corrosive nature of the Republican debate and as well as the actions of the GOP in Congress impeding actions on the CTBT (Nuclear Test Banned Treaty), Law of the Sea Treaty, opposition to the Iran nuclear agreement, and added resources for diplomacy.

Trump has not shown any brilliance in foreign policy, national security, international relations and diplomacy.

He fails to give any impactful and satisfying guidelines through his foreign policy regarding:

    a.   Nuclear Proliferation and balance of power.
    b.   Global trade.
    c.   Global poverty and inequality.
    d.   Building new international institutions and strengthening the

existing ones to fight hunger, disease, illiteracy.
e. Global warming.
f. Human rights.

The Republican camp can only be described as the "Camp of War" and "Climate Change Deniers" but also the camp of those who, without exception, are people of little understanding of how world politics, diplomacy, ensuring security, and the global economy really works. The leader of this camp, is Donald Trump and his approach to national security and foreign affairs is the most radical and ignorant approach the world community has seen in a long time. One of the most interesting and despicable events of 2016 is the love feast between Donald Trump and President Putin. Both love power more than diplomacy.

d. Media feeding frenzy

People will spend more time, especially the Trump lovers, on the media, to interact with their leader. Broadcast media will be selling a lot overseas.

e. Needless deaths in confrontation

More social discontent, frustrations and racism will cause needless deaths in confrontation. There could be riots, possibly a Muslim genocide, public battles between the liberals and the populists on several national issues.

f. Disobedience by his supporters

Donald must change the way he is talking and acting if he becomes President. Otherwise, he won't be able to manage his supporters' expectations in the way they like to interact, flirt with Trump. Trump is down to earth now, because he needs them. If he becomes President, things will change overnight, some of his populist supporters may become disobedient to State law and traditions.

g. Destabilization of domestic politics

Even if becomes President, the dominance and activities of traditional right-wing, extreme right-wing, fascists, racists, populists, KKKs will go up and that will destroy the very mosaic of America's domestic politics, which will only have a chance of recovery once Donald Trump leaves the Oval Office. The Democratic Party will struggle for survival.

h. More harm, global concern

Lack of attention to global warming may become a global issue.

i. More political and economic confrontation in Transatlantic and Transpacific relationships

Trump will definitely have confrontations with the EU and possibly with the NATO. Where the EU is restructuring and adjusting to improve human rights and equality, Trump's country will be going in the opposite direction, causing confrontation and frustration with these countries.

On the Pacific front, he will have a trade war with Japan, China and Korea, which will be another cause of concern for the globe.

j. A constitutional amendment

Trump may well lead a movement toward constitutional changes liberals will hate. But before he does anything like this, the Muslim, Black and Hispanic citizens may well revolt against the US government under Trump at one political point. Then the entire tradition enshrined in the

Constitution could be at risk in US political traditions for a long time.

The point is:

The most compelling force that shaped the birth of the United States comes from John Locke, a 17th century political philosopher who redefined the nature of government. Although he agreed with Hobbes, another political philosopher regarding the self-interested nature of humans, was much more optimistic about their ability to use reason to avoid tyranny.

In his *Second Treatise of Government*, Locke identified the foundation of a legitimate government. According to Locke, a ruler gains authority through the consent of the governed. The duty of that government is to protect the natural rights of the people, which Locke believed to include life, liberty, and property. If the government should fail to protect these rights, its citizens would have the right to overthrow that government. This idea deeply influenced Thomas Jefferson when he drafted the Declaration of Independence.

Dated July 4, 1776, the Declaration of Independence starts with the famous introduction clearly reflected John Locke's social contract theory: "...to secure these rights [Life, Liberty, and the pursuit of happiness], Governments are instituted among men, deriving their just powers from the consent of the governed."

If you punish people who obey the law as a proxy for people who break the law, the law loses its validity and must be remade. Making law in the shadow of conflict is how the Americans have the 2nd amendment. However, the laws and constitution become mockeries and serious marketing tools in an anti-intellectual society that punishes the law abiding citizens for their color, race and religion. That is actually the failure of a constitution.

k. Middle East Peace:

Surprisingly, there may be a serious attempt by the US to bring peace between Israel and Palestine. Israel may get what it has been looking for and the Palestinians get recognition. The cancer of the Middle East may be mitigated forever. If this happens, hate boy Donald Trump will become Playboy Donald Trump, especially in the Muslim world.

In recent interviews and a presidential nominee debate at Miami University, Ted Cruz and Marco Rubio jumped on Donald Trump for favoring US neutrality to pave the way for permanent peace in the Middle East. Their reason was that neutrality will embolden Israel's enemy. Trump explained his position, but still maintains the West's traditional Judeo-Christian view on the existence of Israel.

This means, he is really determined for peace in the Middle East, a bold move by Donald Trump.

But what might trigger fault lines under a President Trump? Let's get some:

1. Rage and revenge from the Wall Street because of his threat to tax the Wall Street.

2. The regrouping and restructuring of Democrats to win a majority in Congress, which would hamstring big man Trump.

3. Failure in the Middle Eastern peace process, which is the only real positive Trump foreign policy that he has shown to the world.

4. Repositioning of ISIS and other radical Islamists to play a chess game with Trump.

5. Not a quick recovery of US economy.

6. Rising disappointment and frustration of right-wing white populists.

7. Faster rise of other regional powers, which will put more pressure on Trump to balance between budget and overspending in the Defense.

8. Riots, genocides and sporadic violence within the US.

9. The effects of scandals revealed about his empire involving government money.

Lots more can trigger his collapse as the President.

Trump is nothing if not overambitious. He will not be the president who embodies an enduring longing for a peaceful, harmonious and stable country. His policies have masked and aggravated structural deficiencies, which are intrinsically connected to make the economy and the democratic establishment languish further. Above all, he can never be an architect of a political construct that seeks America's ultimate purpose in a better-than-possible country created by sound and healthy politics, because his ideologies have serious consequences.

Marco Rubio once said, "Donald Trump is a serious threat to the future of our party, and our country." If Trump wins, a Frankenstein monster will be sitting in the Oval Office.

Trump Cripples America

The election of Obama was a win for equality, freedom and multiculturalism. It was a win of political talent. America was congratulated by the world as a front-runner of democratic light, a world of freedom and equality.

Now, we can't say the same for Trump as a political symbol or a symbol of the victory of American democracy and multiculturalism.

In a nation shaped and defined by a racial hierarchy over the last few decades, Obama's election was very much a radical change, in which a man from one of the nation's less favored class rose to the summit of its political landscape.

And he did so with heavy support from minorities. Asian Americans and Latinos were an important part of Obama's coalition, and black Americans turned out at their highest numbers in the last two elections.

And that was a wakeup call for the right-wing political pundits and politicians, and many timid whites were hyperaware of their racial status and dominance - the loss of the throne. Trump's question about the 'birth certificate' of Obama and his qualification as a president on the ground of foreign birth was just the beginning of a new chapter in US politics.

Market and health reforms are not functioning well. Wealth is changing hands fast in a country where too much liberalization may not have the social and economic conditions necessary to sustain it in a fast-changing situation. This paves the way for conflict with ethnic interests, and it can turn to be violence any time. Trump landed in the middle, and is harvesting it. Can he succeed? If he does, it will be catastrophic for America.

Trump is also the natural and timely outburst of decades-old divisive politics in divided American society - the inevitable outcome of a Republican political strategy that outright strengthened white racial resentment to win elections, in a time while they have decline in wealth and job opportunities.

Trump's political campaign can best be understood through its underlying meaning: its essential nature is neither racism or demagoguery, but is the latest manifestation of the Southern Strategy, which the Republican Party has spent decades developing, in order to bolster its support in the old Confederate states by appeals to racial resentment and white solidarity. It answers why Texan Ted Cruz is so friendly with

Trump. They agree to block a Jewish American candidate from becoming their president as well.

The rise of Donald Trump means the rise of Southern racism, defying the importance of social and political integration among all the races in America. This election opens up the old wounds of racism and violence in the history of two hundred years, and an argument that human beings can never be equal because of their religions, races and colors. It cripples America and embarrasses liberal Americans.

Not only that, he creates the idea that the US can be a divided country: The South and The North creating violence and chaos. If Trump continues the same provocative behavior after winning, he will lead US to divisiveness.

And if this division continues after this election, one day America may be more than one country. The dream for a strong and unified America is over. It is floating as a crippled whale in this election.

But there is no end of these divisive steps Trump uses to attract the racist fringes with, and they are backing him up enthusiastically, which means more yet to come from their side. And this cripples America's future image as a unified, democratic country.

Generally, people think Trump is a strong man for America. That is a wrong perception. Trump is strong only against the Muslims, Barack Obama, the Mexicans and the disabled. On the other hand, he is very weak person who knows how Americans are addicted to drugs and what a burden it is on healthcare. The US has lots of drug cartel problems and Donald completely ignores this significant social cancer. He does not like to mess with the drug lords. That is too dangerous for his brands that he licenses all around the world. In the absence of this political issue, Trump's patriotism for his country looks funny, and America's strength to nominate a person like him is a shame.

Trump's political campaign has already left a durable and deep wound in American history. His provocative discourse of hate has attracted so much attention that paranoid Americans barely even noticed that Senator Ted Cruz had called President Obama "the world's leading financier of radical Islamic terrorism." As a Southern politician, who was born in Calgary, Canada, Ted Cruz did well to win the votes from the right-wing populists and haters.

Trump has created a well-designed fabrication of celebrity, wealth, and alienation to the Republicans, which is more potent than any previously. Trump has deeply polluted American politics, showing its ugly and raucous teeth to the Hispanics, Muslims, Blacks and disabled people.

Racism is a cult-like dark phenomenon that is killing Trump's business empire, and cripples America's image. Even before his political campaign, Trump was sued for deliberate racism. In 1973, the U.S. Justice Department's Civil Rights Division filed a civil rights suit against the Trump organization, charging that it refused to rent to black people. The Urban League had sent black and white testers to apply for apartments in Trump-owned complexes; the whites got the apartments, the blacks didn't. According to court records, four superintendents or rental agents reported that applications sent to the central office for acceptance or rejection were coded by race.

A 1979 *Village Voice* article has been quoted as saying that a rental agent who confessed in the Court of Law Trump instructed him not to rent to black people and to encourage existing black tenants to leave. In 1975, a consent decree described by the head of DOJ's (Department of Justice) housing division as "one of the most far-reaching ever negotiated," required Trump's organization to advertise apartment vacancies in minority papers and list vacancies with the Urban League. The Justice Department subsequently complained that continuing "racially discriminatory conduct by Trump agents has occurred with such frequency that it has created a substantial impediment to the complete enjoyment of equal opportunity."

And the racism continues to the present. After months of echoing the American racist right, Donald Trump was caught retweeting a racist Twitter account.

Trump retweeted the account @WhiteGenocideTM in his official Twitter account. The account, which has claimed "Hitler SAVED Europe" and that "Jews/Israel did 9/11," is named after an increasingly popular racist and anti-Semitic idea that right-wing white populists have worked diligently to push into the mainstream—the idea of "white genocide."

White genocide is the concept that right-wing white populists, far from governing and dominating most of the developed world, are actually being subjected to a genocide that will ultimately wipe out their race. In recent years, the idea has got tremendous momentum and has been spread through something known as the "The Mantra," a 221-word attack on multiculturalism written by Robert Whitaker, who is making a presidential bid this year on the racist American Freedom Party ticket. The Mantra ends with the phrase, "Anti-racist is code word for anti-white."

The re-tweeted tweet has already created considerable attention and energy on the racist right. On Stormfront, the nation's largest white supremacist website, one user nick-named Fading Light said, "[T]his is a GOOD thing. [Trump] willingly retweeted the name. The name was chosen to raise awareness of our plight. Helped propagate it. We should be grateful."

Donald Trump has been caught in another controversy recently after footage emerged of him attending a Sinn Féin fundraising dinner in New York in November 1995, months before the Provisional IRA (Irish Republican Army) broke its ceasefire by bombing London's Canary Wharf.

He was seen shaking hands with Gerry Adams in the Essex House hotel in Manhattan, then they had a meeting.

During his speech, Gerry Adams joked about Sinn Féin playing the "Trump card" before shaking hands with the businessman, who could be seen grinning and waving to the audience. It is mentionable here that Irish terrorism is one of the oldest terrorism in the world.

The Native Americans are not happy with Trump now. What will happen if he becomes president? He is a bad candidate for the Native Americans, because he shows ugly hate toward them, and nastiness toward brown people in general. Will he adhere to the treaties the way Obama did respectfully, for the first time in the history of the USA?

Here is a prime example how Donald treated the American Natives at their native land. About the Native Americans who built a casino close to the Atlantic City Taj Mahal, Trump said, "We don't want them in our neighborhood, do you…" The Native Americans sued and protested against Trump.

Donald Trump hurts old-fashioned multiculturalism, he hurts people's feelings. But who are these people? In the USA, they are the Trump's victims: Muslims, Mexicans, females, poor, disabled, Middle Eastern and Hispanic people. His over-achieving and pompous political branding destroys the grandiosity of the golden old books of the US constitution for which so much blood and sweat were sacrificed. The danger is, feeble American collective social conscience is moving in another direction, rapidly signaling the demise of racial and gender harmony and peace.

In every speech, he says, "I think…" means he is not sure what he is talking about. He is not factual. It shows his weakness and vagueness in detail as a candidate and a non-qualifier as a US President. He doesn't like to play with numbers to give definitive answers. Instead, he relies on his provocative, abstract statements. For an example, in the

University of Miami debate, he said that he would cut waste and corruption to make up a 150 billion dollar deficit in Old Age security. But the statistics say that by cutting waste and corruption, only 3 billion dollar can be saved. How Donald will make up the rest of 147 billion deficit? He didn't have the numbers, or how to get the numbers to make up the whole deficit of 150 dollars. But he insisted he could do it.

Donald blames President Obama regarding Cuba and the nuclear agreement with Iran. He says that best deal, the great deal, the good deal, the intelligent deal was not made. But he falls short of explaining what are those deals, how these deals could have been better. He criticizes with powerful often incendiary and emotional remarks but, often doesn't give any objective or definitive solutions with numbers or facts. It sounds funny and reminds one of a rich layman who proclaims he knows everything because he has the money, but actually he knows very little. Thus he is crippling the standard of an American Presidential candidate. Does he cripple America at the same time? Yes, he has already. Here, he not only cripples the credibility of a Republican Nominee, but also cripples US democratic institutions by his sheer lack of understanding the vital national security issues.

Some may argue for the sake of the argument that other countries and regions are doing much worse. The gross mistakes are here. It opens a flood gate of other arguments. In short, USA is the most powerful and influential country in this world, with its most influential media. She has begot democracy, freedom and equality. So her burden to continue with these values is much greater than of other countries. But the US seriously lags behind.

In his process of abomination, Trump didn't even spare Jeb Bush's wife, who is a bright, decent Mexican. People who are in his world love it, and his Spanish inquisition was a vicious attack in the world of civility and humbleness, for a few millions among around 400 million. He failed to apologize to her to show the chivalry of a man of class and humility. He cripples general American values and decency.

His expressed concern for his country was genuine and is genuine, as it seems always to be. But the provocative methodology of his speeches is not up to a Presidential Candidate or a vintage businessman. How close is he to be a well-seasoned politician? Some say, he's not even close to a minor politician in Idaho. Others want him as their president.

But Trump stays at the top because he uses a classical argumentative structure and classical persuasion to buy his own lettuce in his own garden. Some people have bought it, but even they find it ridiculous. Then the buyers begin to increase in numbers. Doesn't matter to those buyers that he has missed an approach of American values, American long-established political culture and a moral standard.

Some may argue, specially his advisers, Donald has made a paradigm shift in American politics, perhaps in the entire social mosaic, because he doesn't want the Muslims and the Mexicans, because they are bad, they are a security threat. He doesn't care for the values, civility and the US constitution that has been heralding equality and freedom for more than two hundred years. He has his unique business branding transformed to political branding, and against all odds, it is working fantastically in the US society of racism and anti-intellectualism.

However, he has opened his own school that teaches abuse, hatred, disrespect and anti-intellectualism. This is a new, entertaining one, without a sense of good and evil. He has created his own mighty brand name in US politics. After all, he is a successful, brilliant businessman, and one of the best American people have seen so far. He knows the selling tools and the tipping points of winning an argument, if not by sharpness, then by the power of the glamour of his business branding. His tactics are contagious.

"I think that we should definitely disallow any Muslims from coming in. Any of them. The reason is simple: we can't identify what their attitude is," said 75-year-old Charlie Marzka of Myrtle Beach, South Carolina.

Marzka stated that he believes Islam "allows for the killing of people" and said he thinks Muslim culture "is absolutely contrary to our culture."

Marzka is a prime example of US anti-intellectualism. He doesn't feel the need to know Islam and Christianity before making this ignorant comment. No religions allow killing but, adherents to all religions do kill. It has happened hundreds of years ago, and it has happened during the two world wars, and it still happens in the Middle East and in some parts of Africa. Whose claim is more powerful - faith or life? Whose claim is more dominating - ideology or humanity? We are stuck in the middle.

To Trump, all the religions are not equal, and neither are people. He has his own school of equality and freedom for his emotional supporters of anti-intellectualism, and they pose a bigger threat to US democracy than Donald Trump. It cripples the idea of globalization and one single global family.

But the fact is his controversial attitudes come as Trump's poll numbers have continued to rise with the latest national CNN/ORC poll showing Trump leading the field of Republican presidential contenders by 20 points with 36% of support.

And winning an argument? It can be done in so many entertaining ways, even in genuine ways. Ordinary people do less care about the ways, they care for the fiery brilliance, the outcome of it to charm them, to entertain them as does the funny eloquence of Barack Obama.

Trump will cripple America further if he wins. His lack of understanding of national sensitive issues like nuclear weapons is a prime example.

Trump's Terrifying Nuke Answer at the Republican Nominee Debate, summarized below, should have ended his political campaign. But it didn't, because:

1. His mother tongue is English.
2. Extreme anti-intellectualism persists in USA.
3. He has a crisp, sharp branding.
4. Racists, right-wing populists backs him up blindly.

In the debate, right-wing radio host Hugh Hewitt's question: "Mr. Trump, Dr. Carson just referenced the single most important job of the president, the command, the control and the care of our nuclear forces. And he mentioned the triad. The B-52s are older than I am. The missiles are old. The submarines are aging out. It's an executive order. It's a commander-in-chief decision. What's your priority among our nuclear triad?"

Hewitt is suggesting the technologies Americans use to deliver a nuclear attack are too old, and asking Trump what his priority would be when it comes to maintaining them.

This was Trump's response after a long pause: "Well, first of all, I think we need somebody absolutely that we can trust, who is totally responsible, who really knows what he or she is doing. That is so powerful and so important."

In the answer, Trump's first sentence is somewhat reasonable. Americans *do* need someone they can trust, who is totally responsible, who knows what he or she is doing when it comes to taking charge of their nuclear arsenal. But this wasn't an introduction to a fuller answer explaining why he knows what he's doing or what his plans are. To Trump, that *was* the substantive answer. "Make America Great Again" is a perfectly fine slogan if Trump has a plan to make America great again, but with him, the slogan is the entire agenda, a selling tool. There is no plan.

How do people know Trump is responsible enough to handle America's nuclear arsenal? He went on:

"And one of the things that I'm frankly most proud of is that in 2003, 2004, I was totally against going into Iraq because you're going to destabilize the Middle East. I called it. I called it very strongly. And it was very important."

Trump is deliberately lying. He did not, in fact, strongly object to the Iraq War before it began. But even if he was against the Iraq War, that doesn't qualify him to control and maintain the world's largest collection of nuclear bombs. He continued, "I opposed the war, marching with signs and everything. And please believe me when I tell you I have no business anywhere near a bomb with the power to evaporate a city."

Trump wasn't done yet. "But we have to be extremely vigilant and extremely careful when it comes to nuclear. Nuclear changes the whole ballgame. Frankly, I would have said get out of Syria; get out—if we didn't have the power of weaponry today. The power is so massive that we can't just leave areas that 50 years ago or 75 years ago we wouldn't care. It was hand-to-hand combat."

Again, Trump is right, in a childlike way. The Americans do have to be careful with nuclear; it does change the whole ballgame. But these are generalities borne out of ignorance. In 145 words Trump has yet to approach anything remotely like an answer to Hewitt's question. He hasn't said yet what his priority would be when it comes to maintaining or upgrading American nukes. He hasn't even said what his principles would be. But surely that's coming soon, right?

You know what? Let's just finish the exchange.

Trump: "The biggest problem this world has today is not President Obama with global warming, which is inconceivable, this is what he's saying. The biggest problem we have is nuclear - nuclear proliferation and having some maniac, having some madman go out and get a nuclear weapon. That's in my opinion that is the single biggest problem that our country faces right now."

Hewitt: "Of the three legs of the triad, though, do you have a priority? I want to go to Sen. Rubio after that and ask him."

Trump: "I think—I think, for me, nuclear is just the power, the devastation is very important to me."

The devastation is very important to him, to redirect them to any religion or race. That flailing nonsense is the best Trump can manage at any time for his targeted audience, millions of them, who love him, who love America. A reasonably well-informed eighth grader could have come up with something better.

The problem isn't simply that Trump doesn't have detailed plans to make sure America's nuclear weapons are safely maintained. The problem is that he doesn't understand even the most basic premise of a relatively simple question. He couldn't muster, "I'll make sure we have the most modern, best nuclear arsenal the world has ever seen," because he didn't know what he was being asked. Maybe, he does not know what "nuclear triad" means.

It is all flirting and entertaining rather than being factual. President Obama said, "He is scapegoating."

And handing over the nuclear codes to a man with the comprehension skills of Donald J. Trump in a serious security issue. Do you honestly believe he would understand the consequences of using them? Trump is obsessed with tough-guy machismo. How much provocation does he need to press that button? How will he behave with other world leaders? How will he handle other national security issues? But the fact is, Trump's supporters will follow him blindly even if he starts a nuclear war without understanding the dangers. America is in danger.

This moment should be the beginning of the end for his campaign. Just like all the other moments should have been.

Here is another example of Trump's inability to deliver the correct information. Before the New York Primary, he was in Buffalo trying to invoke the attacks on the World Trade Center, describing the courage he saw there. There was just one small problem—he mixed up the date.

"Because I was down there, and I watched our police and our firemen down on 7/11, down at the World Trade Center, right after it came down and I saw the greatest people I have ever seen in action," Trump said.

The attack took place on September 11, 2001.

But this gross incompetency did not put him down. Rather, he became stronger, because he is entertaining with his power of words, and the anti-intellectualism of the US voters and supporters, and because there is a rising group in US with a sentiment against the Muslims. Almost the same sentiment that both Bush Presidents used to go to war in the Middle East.

Trump hasn't taken back any of the racist, ignorant, stupid things he's said over the course of the campaign, and he certainly won't admit to making a mistake. But his inability to muster ten remotely sensible words about what he would do as president with the most destructive collection of weapons in the history of mankind should be an automatic disqualifier for the presidency. It should be, but hasn't been because of the quality of the voters.

This wasn't the year that Trump burst into public consciousness, nor was it the year Trump got political—he's had presidential ambitions since at least 1999. Rather, 2015 was the year Donald Trump held the Republican Party hostage, and the rest of America captive.

Here are the few things that happened quickly to boost Trump and his political branding:

New York attorney general Eric Schneiderman is the latest target of Donald Trump's vitriol. He's leading a $40 million lawsuit against Trump University, accusing the professional development program of persistent fraud, illegal and deceptive conduct, and violating federal consumer protection law. Instead of remaining silent, as some publicists would advise in the face of such a major lawsuit, Trump fired back, calling Schneiderman "a political hack looking to get publicity." Donald Trump never stops and he has his own way to deliver things.

Donald Trump is a real estate tycoon, reality TV show star and potential political candidate—and he's one of the most derided men in American history. He didn't stumble into this reputation. In fact, he's built his personal brand on being provocative. With almost 2.7 million Twitter followers, and more than 780,000 likes on Facebook, Donald Trump thrives on controversy, attracting a huge audience by churning out vitriol about everything from the rising power of China to the plummeting reputation of baseball star Alex Rodriguez. Donald Trump has his name on a lot of high-rise real estate, but none of it compares to the towering brand he has constructed by spewing rage.

Of course, vitriol is a two-way street. Donald Trump invites it, knowing well that his unrestrained attacks of others brew the controversy that surrounds him. He knows the consequences, which in the past have been minimal where he is totally backed up by US media.

And every time Trump said something, either right or wrong, people liked him because it was entertaining, and a few checked what was underneath his motivation. What did it matter to Trump if Jon Stewart used him as nightly cannon fodder? It was, as we now say, good for the brands.

But under his brands, another Trump has been growing over the decades with the support of the right-wing mainstream and the media and under the camouflage of a unique branding, and nice and smooth talking. Trump's blithe contempt has many targets. Blacks are one of them.

In 1989, Trump put an ad in the *Daily News* about the Central Park jogger rape case, in which he stated that the "criminals of every age" who had been arrested twelve days earlier—five African-American and Hispanic teen-agers—were "crazed misfits," part of "roving bands." "BRING BACK THE DEATH PENALTY," the ad read. "BRING BACK OUR POLICE!"

Years of trial after, these black people were found not guilty, acquitted of all charges, since it turned out that someone else had committed the crime, and the young men were released from prison.

Their release infuriated Trump. Then he wrote an unapologetic op-ed for the newspaper in which he called the city's push for restitution payments to the black men "a disgrace." He made it clear that, to him, their lives were nothing. Besides, "These young men do not exactly have the pasts of angels." A GOP presidential nominee with such a record indicates it is the wind of change, unhealthy and uneasy.

Trump has been among the country's foremost "birthers," constantly prompting the idea, against all evidence, that Barack Obama was born in some other country and, therefore, is constitutionally unable to hold the office. That was actually the beginning of his undeclared political campaign.

Trump's political and ideological attacks have generally been promotional brand extensions, lasting only as long as they were, in his view, good for business; the whole game might end well before the first snows in New York. But what will happen to his empire? He will be considered as a con man who made so many tremors in US politics that the KKK, fascists and right-wing populists in America. Things will not be easy for his branding.

His arrival in this election campaign was indecent. Usually, when a candidate announces a run, it comes through decent press releases and some positive notes to the potential voters. But in Trump's case, it was just the opposite, because American society has changed a lot. Here are a few unusual actions heralding his entry to the contest, which have crippled America's long established political traditions and norms:

1. Vilification of Muslims. In the first week of February, 2016, President Obama visited one mosque in Maryland. He said, referring to Donald Trump, that an insult to Islam to an insult to all the religions. His short and bold remark has crippled the credibility of the Republican Party, which is still trying to get out of Donald's mess. But Trump came roaring back with his vengeance during the Miami University Republican debate, where he said, "1.6 billion Muslims are terrorists" and that includes Barack Obama as well, who has, unfortunately the middle name of Hussein.

2. Hatred for the Mexicans. Aggressive, incendiary comments to attract increasing far right and extremists' groups and individuals among US voters.

3. Feeding on ignorant, frightened and xenophobic US voters. They think when some terrorists are Muslims, then all Muslims are terrorists. They are not able to understand that Islam is a religion, neither a race nor a nation. What they find that some Mexicans are rapists, then all Mexicans are rapists as Trump has already successfully brainwashed them. We can't blame them, they are hardworking people who pay taxes, but

unfortunately, one third of them don't know where Canada is. We even can't blame these people, because when US Vice President candidate Sarah Palin received a phone call from a Quebec radio station (with a French accent because Quebec is bilingual) in Canada, she thought she had got a call from France. It is very unjust to blame common US people, because this is the way it is in the most powerful, hegemonic country named USA. They have their own world, and what that do is right, because might is right.

4. Using his business brand, entrepreneurship, and celebrity stance, he is poised to harvest more on achieving his goal in US politics.

After Bush's presidency, the USA has been slow in creating new active wars. US tax-payers' money is saved, young soldiers' lives are saved, their families are not broken, and the US Federal Reserve is printing less US Treasury Bills to borrow money to accept the cost of wars. Obama has done a good job for the majority of the Americans.

What happened in US society in 2008? The end of Bush's legacy? Did we forget? Yes, we tend to. We may learn lessons from the past but we very soon forget them. The politicians know this well, which is why they are so good at manipulating public opinion.

Trump has repeatedly shown his political irresponsibility, but surprisingly this is not a negative for the lowest common denominator of American electorate, because they are extremely anti-intellectual. Their xenophobic, hateful politics aren't new. But the American people haven't seen anything like this in mainstream presidential politics for some time. Two examples in the past century are segregationist George Wallace's 1968 bid that was rooted in the restoration of the Southern Racial Segregationist Jim Crow-era laws against the Blacks, and Herbert Hoover's 1924 campaign where preachers in the South roused up anti-Catholic sentiments against Al Smith, the first Roman Catholic presidential candidate ever nominated by a major party.

And this answers why Donald Trump is so much disrespectful to Roman Catholic Pope Francis of The State of Vatican City.

"I think that the pope is a very political person," Trump said. He had a message for Pope Francis ahead of the pope's trip to pray with the migrants along the Mexican border: "You don't get it" he continued, "I think he doesn't understand the problems that our country has". We can't blame Donald boy, he is right in bisecting between the religious grandiosity and the harsh reality in national and economic crisis.

On February 18, 2016, Trump becomes embroiled in a dispute with Pope Francis again, who critiqued the candidate's immigration plans as "not Christian".

Trump hits back with a warning: "If and when the Vatican is attacked by ISIS, which as everyone knows is ISIS's ultimate trophy, I can promise you that the Pope would have only wished and prayed that Donald Trump would have been president."

Almost 50 years after George Wallace's bid, the Americans have found another one in Donald Trump, and his timing is perfect. While Trump might not be popular with a large segment of the Republican Party, many voters no longer feel connected to Washington and its entrenched political class. With his populist streak, Trump has already appealed to these voters. In return, Trump is demeaning American multi-culturalism, social integration, racial peace and harmony. Above all, has struck at the very institution of democracy.

Trump has shown the world the dark side of US politics and social mechanism. He has exhumed the old stinks of racism, hate, and segregation, buried deep in US history.

Trump has broken just about every rule of conventional campaigning. He has been short on policy diagnosis and prescription, and long on provocation. Yet, he still reigns supreme atop the Republican field, which shows that what Republicans like the most is embarrassing to the liberals.

Americans have made him unstoppable. Trump bounds onstage to raucous applause from large crowds of Americans. American democracy has allowed him to make such provocative remarks. It is the American political system that has made him so close to being a fascist. He is an embarrassment to the politically-aware American liberals, even the Republicans.

Even Republican Collin Powel has said that Trump is hurting America's image abroad. But it is too early for Powel to condemn Donald, because the history of success depends on the unified lies by the victors, and you must give enough time to the victors to redefine history in their own image.

And the wait is even longer when Trump has set up a new boundary for political morality in the USA like some of his predecessors, who did partially, where humanity is at stake.

Politics is a complex and dangerous game of heartless manipulation, wealth, and powerful oration. To be successful in politics, one brave heart must have these elements, otherwise be in the Guantanamo Bay or in an animal's farm.

Trump's political campaign, using provocation and manipulation, will illuminate the hearts of his loyal supporters even if he fails and their thriving will continue making US a difficult country. Trump's father was a self-promoter who dispersed discounts in his balloons flying over Coney Island. His son offers only toxic gas. And both work in fast changing American society. They have unique means of success.

Here is one example of Trump's meanness and indecency. He held a rally in Manchester, New Hampshire, before the Primary, where he merrily copied a woman in the crowd who called Ted Cruz a pussy. Twenty-four hours later, Donald Trump won the New Hampshire primary in a landslide. America is a strange place, the place of Old Puritanism that has nothing left that is good and decent.

The US media, which has grown used to covering more Trump than Bernie Sanders, delighted in the moment along with him, because his indecent comment was funny, and it meant much more clicks, takes, traffic, twits and money. Money! But it was more than that. It was the frontrunner for the Republican nomination for president showing off the demagogue's instinct for amplifying the angriest voice in the mob for his personal gain. American people love it.

It's so amusing to watch that it's easy to lose sight of how terrifying it really is. Trump is the most dangerous major candidate for president in memory. He plays an immoral game with his disrespect for truth, and brings out the worst in American culture, dogmatic and problematic for a civilization.

But wait. This is all about politics. Donald Trump is not yet the president of the USA. He is still a businessman, with his business empire dotted on the world map. But what is more important to Donald Trump and his advisors: his business strength, or political gains, or both?

World conscience is not dead yet. Outrage is spewing in- and outside of the USA. The world still needs political and financial leadership from USA. But if a popular, highly supported US president is mad, it is time to reassess our entire existence.

Some are saying, "We want the old American values, we don't want anything to do with Donald Trump." You can't hold on to peoples' thinking, you can't hold on to people's craving for freedom, you can't hold on to peoples' craving for equality. The moral judgment of right or wrong is still there, fighting the dark jaws of degeneration, if not in the land of New Puritanism.

Trump's dilemma is he is in the middle of a political campaign, where backtracking on statements can be seen as being self-destructive. So while an apology now may save his business, it may hurt his presidential ambitions. He is a crackerjack in abomination created by own strategy.

"It's served him well in his personal endeavors and business," Howard Stern stated. "But what we find is that brands, politicians and businesses can quickly go off the deep end."

He can't apologize because he has so many issues to apologize about, and he is not the man of apology. But he is getting more civil in his speech as he is closing in to the general election. Doesn't matter, if the Republican Party wants a brighter future must distance from Trump in supporting him.

Now he is sharpening his horns to lock with the Clintons', who were once his friends. Hopefully, he will show civility when criticizing them, specially opening the old wounds regarding Monica Lewinsky.

What he has started, he must finish. The hate and violence that he has inflicted in US voters' minds are sustainable for a while. And this hate is contagious and now around the world. Trump knew well that his mission was very possible. His grandfather and father taught him, winning at any cost is the bottom line, while the sense of right or wrong is a loser's virtue.

The Republican Party, which used to be hawkish, is now a party of demagoguery and racism, and Trump has been dominating right in the middle. And saying something against Trump in the Republican Party is like holding a live grenade in front of your face. Scary! He is coming to get you!

Sadly, Obama's, presidency backfired for 1.6 billion Muslims. Now all the Muslims are terrorists, all the Muslims hate America - according to Donald Trump.

The reason Obama is responsible for the rise of this Donald Trump is that Obama is not 'radical' 'liar' not a 'warmonger.' Instead, he is a center-leftist in the Democratic Party. Some Republicans say Obama is a disciple of American communist guru Frank Marshall.

Here, Trump has not only got the growing anti-Muslim votes in USA, but tactfully he has aroused millions of Muslim haters around the world, who now like to spew hate and provocation on Muslims. Trump has backstabbed the Muslim religion and thus has made USA a Muslim hater. Democracy falters, and without pride, sadly.

This has happened because of a deep and unnegotiable anti-intellectualism of America. Otherwise, Americans would have understood in a timely fashion that the US is not endangered by Muslim radicals, but by Trump himself. When they will understand, maybe it will be too late. The loss will be irreversible: certain races will be more alienated and racial tension and hatred will be growing alarmingly, crippling freedom and harmony around the world.

Not only does Trump lead a fascist movement of almost exclusively disaffected whites, but he wins his strongest support in states and counties with the highest degree of racial polarization, especially in the Southern states. And when he declared his run on TV, he said that undocumented Mexicans are rapists. His comment was very strategic to get the right-wing support from these states where these undocumented Mexicans are one of their major problems. And his strategy worked perfectly in the first hour of his campaign; he had already achieved millions of votes in the South. Even though this political trick worked well, and recruited the rage of the Southerners who were overlooked on this Mexican issue, it has crippled America's image overall,

Among white voters, higher levels of racial resentment have been shown to be associated with greater support for Trump. This is a big problem for America, whether he wins or not. He has exacerbated racial hatreds and divisions for years, still he doesn't care.

Muslims in US have the reason that it was a gross mistake for Americans to vote for Barack Hussein Obama even though he has been their best president since Kennedy, perhaps since Eisenhower. Now Hispanics, Blacks, disabled people, and especially the Muslims are paying for this mistake, because Trump is winning and has ignited hatred for the Muslims including his president who is partly Muslim because he has a middle Muslim name – the Republican Propaganda. Obama is a pure Christian. You can't get away from the fact that, for American white racists, it does not matter what you think or how well you do. America has never had democracy for all, but only for the white Anglo-Saxon Europeans. Others, are scared, nervous and with reason. First the Irish, then the Italians, then the Japanese went through repression in democratic and free America.

Immigration tactics during the 19th century focused on similarly erroneous concerns about the criminality and inherent "otherness" of immigrants, for example:

1. Benjamin Franklin notoriously referred to American Germans as "stupid" and "swarthy."

2. President Millard Fillmore waged the second most successful third-party presidential campaign of all time on a platform devoted to keeping "un-American" Catholics out of the country.

3. Franklin Roosevelt established internment camps for the Japanese-Americans during WWII.

Trump follows in their footprints when he argues that Muslims carry ID cards, and Syrian refugees be monitored in a federal database.

The targets of hate are being extended. Get ready. Liberal Americans have already threatened to move to Canada for their safety.

Google searches on "How can I move to Canada" have increased in frequency, and stayed number one for a while after Trump's win on Super Tuesday during the first week of March, 2016. Many American people are trying to escape a potential Trump presidency.

Trump knows well about his strategy and plan, that dirty, racist, demagoguery comments are lethally working for him. For his empire and branding, what he has been doing is very risky, and may prove to be devastating.

Generally, people will ask: how can a presidential candidate make so many errors, before the election? What will happen then after the Presidential election if he wins? So at this point, Trump has only one choice, to continue as he has, which will take him, his party and country to another level, where a big monster is waiting for the Muslims, the Hispanics and the Blacks.

Eroding democracy caused by the emergence of Trump in the US political spectrum as a racist demagogue is threatening human rights, equality and freedom. And what you believe human rights to be are dependent on what you believe human beings are. Actually, Trump has put the Republican Party in a collision course with the US constitution. His political campaign should have been subject to democratic legitimacy and accountability of a national public safety commission, and challenged outright. This did not happen, because the USA with its mighty media and administration is crippled already with right-wing fascistic elements.

These emotional Republicans actually vote and have overwhelmingly sided with this billionaire-turned-actor-

turned-writer-turned-vicious-politician-turned-I-love-you-sir
in nearly every primary election. Now what chance would he
have against either a woman candidate feminist who supports
Obama-care, or a Jewish socialist reformer who wants free
tuition at public universities? Or is Trump's campaign an
opening "act" of a four-year political tragedy in the making?
Can America absorb this shock and survive as the strongest
nation on earth?

Trump has even created problems among the
Republican leadership and candidates. He is unstoppable
anywhere, because he is everywhere, under someone's skin.
Even the Republican candidates are waiting for his fall, if not
that of his empire. No wonder many of the other candidates in
this race are surprisingly disinclined to criticize Trump. They
anticipate the political risk and a fiery response from Trump
that can ruin their run for the party nomination.

However, they hope that, assuming this star fades in
his race, they may be in a position to take over his former
supporters. That helps explain why Senator Ted Cruz of Texas,
amongst others, has been happy to call Trump his "friend."
Few have been as courageous as Perry who called Trump a
"cancer" within the GOP, complaining that the business
magnate offers nothing more than "a toxic mix of
demagoguery, mean-spiritedness, and nonsense." Some
Americans can see a ray of hope in these leaders while US
political culture is rapidly degenerating. This is a great
disappointment for this world and for the Republican Party.

After Sarah Palin, another damage has been done to
the Republican Party, the Americans have worse from the
Apple Street Mogul, whose harm is long lasting and strategic.
The Re-publican Party is crazy and unsettled. They are just
counting the short term achievements, destroying their future.
The policy makers are seriously biased.

The only optimism for humanity in this Trump circa
is many Republicans now hate and fear Trump and some of

them have reacted positively to his attack, because Trump signals the end of old, fundamental values to make America great again in his own way.

Even former first lady Laura Bush blasted the GOP in the first week of April, 2016 in a meeting flanked by her daughters Barbara and Jenna.

Well respected in the GOP Laura Bush said, "I want our next president—whoever he or she might be—to be somebody who is interested in women in Afghanistan and who will continue US policies… that we continue to do what we're committed to do as a country. That's who I want—or the kind of people that will do that and will pay attention to our history, and know what's happened before and know specifically how we can continue to do the good things that we do around the world."

Her daughter Jenna said about her young daughter, "I worry about her future."

Although Bush didn't flat-out endorse any candidates, she hinted that she was part of an ever-growing group of Republicans who are considering voting for Clinton because they will do anything not to vote for Trump.

Laura Bush and her daughter resonate the common concern about Donald Trump, who is a sexist, believes in male dominance. The grandiosity of equality and freedom of American Constitution falters in this campaign. Once protection of civil liberties and civil rights was perhaps the most fundamental political value in American society.

The existing inconsistencies, contradictions and confusion won't soon vanish from US politics. But in today's politically poisoned climate, righteousness or "political correctness" is at its record low and historical political reality falls hard with a bang. Each side, whether "liberal" or "conservative," Republican or Democrat, behaves as if it has a monopoly on historical truth. The fear that the existence of their version of America is threatened sows divisions and hatred and explains why love of one's own country has become a double-edged sword, dividing people when it might unite. And Trump is the pioneer of this division that cripples the US politically and culturally.

Donald Trump is an embarrassment for this civilization. But more pathetic is, Trump is only articulating what other Republicans are actually thinking. In turn, Trump is acting, sometimes, as its puppet.

America has a system, a well-calculated and disciplined one, which rewards only those who win at any cost, even over humanity and human lives. America is a country of winners, built on winners. This is scary for humanity.

If Trump wins, the very definition of democracy will change in America. The government will be of the ASEA, by the ASEA and for the ASEA. ASEA means Anglo-Saxon European Americans. The extreme right wing, which has been dormant for years as political fringes, will try hard to dictate the nature of society, the administration and the economy. The very multicultural mosaic of American society will change, maybe forever.

There is no universal agreement about what constitutes politics, but there are some core questions relating to a government and how authoritative decisions are made in a society. One of the questions is: on what principles is the government based on? If we analyze Donald Trump's political campaign, and his and his followers' ideology, we cannot find any basic principles that constitute a safe model for the political history of the USA. The GOP does not have the process for refining this missing point and its other political institutions and behavior. Hence, American democracy shows the dark side of its political mechanism.

As a nation, America is already crippled by the cost of many major wars and severe wealth polarization, and what is left over after Obama's administration Trump is going to cripple it further, making US almost a failed country, a modern

Empire in decline. Certainly, this is good news for the rogue countries. ISIS can consider that the US is not actually for real anymore.

American democracy will not radiate any rays of lights for a while.

Will Trump's Empire Survive?

After showing and nurturing the very tenets of fascism, totalitarianism, provocation, hatred and violence, Trump must wait to see how his empire collapses if he fails.

The GOP may distance itself from Trump if he fails, because he did not work well for them. They will clean up the house by dumping Donald and announcing their naïve mistakes and new strategies for great America, but probably not his followers. His brand will get a tremendous hit. At least, some of his brand users will think about the fascist and other disturbing elements that he had shown in this political campaign and sown for the future. They will probably dump Trump brands for their survival and growth, and that will be a severe blow to Trump's brand as well as his empire.

Still, some optimists think that even if Trump doesn't win the presidency, his brand will still be a powerful and lucrative money-making machine for him. However, it probably will look very different, and appeal to very different audiences, than it did prior to his campaign.

Trump Entertainment Resorts Inc.'s Taj Mahal in Atlantic City, New Jersey will survive as part of billionaire Carl Icahn's Empire under a bankruptcy protection restructuring plan approved by a federal judge.

"The Taj will remain open," U.S. Bankruptcy Judge Kevin Gross said at a hearing in Wilmington, Delaware. "And it will be a successful venture."

Trump Entertainment, which also owns the closed Trump Plaza, adds to Icahn's gaming venues in the downtrodden seaside town, joining the Tropicana, which the investor acquired out of bankruptcy five years ago.

Lenders controlled and dominated by Icahn provided Trump Entertainment $20 million in bankruptcy financing to help fund operations until the turnaround plan takes effect.

Under the bankruptcy plan, the Icahn lender group gets control of both casinos by converting about $292 million of debt into equity in the reorganized company. The Icahn group will also provide $13.5 million to fund the Taj Mahal after it exits court protection.

The casino owner was able to eliminate most opposition to the plan, striking a great deal with unsecured creditors recently and with founder Donald Trump.

"I'm happy to have reached a deal with Carl—a friend and someone who my father and I have great respect for," Ivanka Trump, who helped negotiate the agreement, said in an e-mail. "The Trump Taj Mahal will, in short order, be greatly reinvested in and brought up to the high standard of luxury consistent with our brand and required under our license agreement."

It is notable here that Donald Trump and his company haven't been involved in running the Atlantic City casinos for about 10 years. Trump still holds a number of gaming licenses in the U.S., but doesn't own or operate any casinos.

But the fall of his empire will be difficult because Trump has already made a lot of money that he can inject in his business. "A lot of people don't think that he made money in Atlantic City," says one source close to Trump who asked to remain anonymous. "They say, 'Donald Trump went bankrupt in Atlantic City.' But the truth is that he made a ton of money there."

Michael Cohen, Trump Organization Executive Vice President and Special Counsel to Donald Trump, confirmed that Trump is considering returning to the Boardwalk in full force.

"I can confirm that Mr. Trump is looking at Trump Entertainment Resorts in Atlantic City," says Cohen. "But he's doing so cautiously."

After the election, if he fails, Donald may not be able to return to the Boardwalk in full force because he has been portrayed by lot of Americans as a fascist demagogue. If his reputation as a solid businessman is destroyed, he may lose his empire piece by piece.

His reputation is also tarnished abroad. A half of his capital worth is goodwill and endorsement, which is more than three billion dollars in economic value within different geographical locations. Some foreign investors may be waiting for the election result. If Trump fails, they may dump his licensing, even breaking contractual obligations.

One condominium tower in Vancouver, Canada has been under construction endorsed by Donald Trump. Someone has already suggested to remove Donald's name from the tower because of his derogatory comments about Spanish Mexicans and Muslims.

In the recent Miss Universe Pageant Show in California, the Mexican contestant threatened not to attend the show unless Donald Trump is kicked out. And Trump was kicked out.

Macy has already announced it will phase out Trump's line of branded menswear, and PVH Corp., the company that produced the shirts and ties, declared its intention for "wind down" its business relationship with Trump. The mattress company Serta announced it would stop selling its Trump Home series mattress. One company in the

Middle East has pulled everything with the tag 'Donald Trump' from its shelves.

Donald Trump had once threatened to cancel over 700 million pounds of planned investments in golf courses in Scotland, had Britain slapped him with a travel ban.

The threat from Trump, owner of two golf courses in his mother's homeland of Scotland, comes as British lawmakers prepare to hold a debate on a petition signed by over half a million people calling for him to be barred from the country after his proposal to stop Muslims entering the United States.

"Any action to restrict travel would force The Trump Organization to immediately end these and all future investments we are currently contemplating in the United Kingdom," the group said in a statement.

The Trump Organization said in a statement that a ban would result in him pulling developments worth 500 million pounds at a golf complex in northeastern Scotland, and a 200-million pound revamp at a resort in the country's southwest.

The debate in the British House of Commons, held on Jan. 18, 2016, ended without a vote. Only interior minister Theresa May can issue an order banning entry into Britain, and Prime Minister David Cameron has said he does not favor barring Trump. Theresa May did not pass the ban. Trump survived but not without being humiliated.

Trump's comments on banning Muslims from entering the United States in December prompted international outrage and led to him being stripped of two Scottish honorary positions.

The proud, half-Scottish billionaire's once-harmonious relationship with Scotland soured further when he was blocked by a top Scottish court in his bid to stop a wind farm being constructed near his Trump International Golf Links course in Aberdeen.

NBC has already cancelled the contract for his famous reality show *The Apprentice,* on the basis of his derogatory comments of the Muslims and the Mexicans. This was a severe blow to Donald and his Trump Empire. He threatened to take legal action against NBC as expected, but in real life nothing has happened yet.

This is a milestone for the USA, the freedom and liberty incubator and protector around the globe. NBC has done an amazing job, indicating the USA is not morally broke yet.

Things are closing in around Donald Trump. Is he scared of losing his empire? Is winning the US Presidency a compensation for his business loss? Or is he gambling politically and trying to win the votes of the people who don't like the Muslims and the Hispanics? What will happen if he wins the Presidency? That will open a brand new door for his business. New power and money will be added to his empire. If not that, then he can try to a have a stimulus package for his troubling business, which employs thousands of people.

And that brand, according to new data published in POLITICO MAGAZINE for the first time, is taking a major hit in the wake of his presidential campaign.

Trump has built a distinctive trademark over the course of decades in public life, turning his own wealth, glamorous lifestyle and personality into emblems of his multi-billion-dollar company through endless self-promotion. It worked perfectly for him until he landed in the presidential campaign.

It is questionable now, during this political journey, how much importance Trump gives to the relation between personal reputation and brand. Trump considers this reputation alone a hugely significant part of his business, which makes his name the single most significant item in his portfolio. Trump's brand was also his first great advantage as a presidential candidate, giving him the name recognition and the gloss of success.

But Trump as a candidate has ascended to the top of the polls and he is staying there, blowing his trumpet. It seems good for his political career but in business, the opposite has happened to Trump the brand.

His empire is losing its business. A survey of American consumer opinion in December, 2015, handled by the BAV Consulting division of advertising and marketing giant Young & Rubicam: the largest and longest running study of brands in the world established the fact that since Donald Trump's run for president, the Trump brand has lost the confidence of the consumers. They tend to stay away from his empire. Its association, the golden traits Trump has long promoted as an inevitable essence of his business is diminishing fast. Bad news for Trump and his descendants.

Furthermore, in US consumer categories such as "dazzling upper class" "prestigious," and "glamorous," with a very high income level, the Trump name has plummeted. Within the same consumers group, it is also losing its new connection with the very terms "a business leader," and "innovative."

And this rapid loss has been incurred in less than a year. This brand has been a survey-subject for BAV Consulting's regular surveys for over a decade, and has never before experienced such a fast drop in business reputation. It is the kind of change that usually follows a big corporate scandal, like a product recall, financial misconduct, or reputation and good-will disaster. But in Trump's case it's a man's personality that is in play in the domain of harsh and risky politics.

Trump's empire has taken some hits already among his target consumer base: the luxury, or "aspirational" market of those making over $100,000 a year. The wealthiest respondents in the BAV survey, whose yearly incomes is over

$150,000, judge Trump the harshest. In this group, as measured by BAV's consumer opinion index, Trump's reputation for being "obliging" and "upper class" has declined by more than 50 percent since the outset of the campaign, followed by "leader" with a 41 percent decline and "prestigious" down by 39 percent. The next lower income level, who are making between $100,000 and $150,000 a year, wasn't much kinder, with a 56 percent decline for "obliging," and a 45 percent decline in "prestigious" and a 38 percent drop for "upper class."

In interviews conducted before the campaign, Trump's children, who work in his companies, acknowledged that their father is the brand and that he will dominate its marketing for the rest of his days. "He became synonymous with success and aspiration," noted daughter Ivanka Trump. "That is still at the core of what the brand is today."

But the challenge of a brand future clouded by his father's polarizing views was on Donald Trump. Jr.'s mind in 2014, long before his father declared his run for president. "If you're asking, 'do I think that he knows he's a polarizing guy?' Yes. The answer is 100-percent," Donald Jr. said. "He will be out there, and he will question these things in a way that you don't see anyone doing today—or certainly not anyone that has a brand. ... There could be potentially ramifications to his business for taking these stances."

How serious will these consequences be for the survival of his empire? We might never know: as head of a privately held company, free of financial obligations to shareholders, Donald Trump has no reason to disclose the financial hit he takes due to his controversial campaign. Still, it is worth noting that these kinds of blows can be massive: During the dot-com crash, firms that fell from grace took multi-billion- dollar "goodwill" write-offs. AOL noted a $99 billion loss in goodwill. Worldcom's was $45 billion.

Donald Trump's fortune is counted in the billions. He will very likely remain wealthy and comfortable—a success as he defines it—for the rest of his days because of his well-set-up industry competitiveness, and innovation dynamics. But those, like his children, who may have counted on the brand to sustain them further into the future, cannot be so certain.

Then again, they could move into the part of the retail consumer market where no real damage has been done: perhaps a Trump brand of smokes, or maybe canned meat that most of his white populist voters will love to buy.

Donald Trump's personal brand — his name alone — has always been an integral part of his success. Branding experts by *WhoWhatWhy* felt that this astronomically high value for a five-letter name seems accurate in comparison with real estate brands of similar success.

To see the enormous value of Trump's brand, one need to look no further than the success he has had in the campaign for US president so far. Many Trump supporters have made it clear that their support for the candidate comes from a belief in his personal integrity and business skills more than in his policy proposals.

And this is a vital point in his political campaign. While other candidates - either Republicans or Democrats, are discussing and debating with numbers, Donald Trump is absolutely the opposite. He does not come up with any numbers or facts, just fiery, provocative rhetoric or simply "I'll make a great deal of it, I'll make a best deal of it." His followers buy this, because their leader has a long track record of successful deal making.

Making Trump's brand the focus of his campaign may have led to polling success in the short term, but as experts in brand marketing suggest, it may pose a large risk if things go sour for him in the election.

"If I was buying stock in Trump's brand, I'd probably want to sell it now," Ian Stephens, owner and managing partner at Saffron Brand Consultants, told *WhoWhatWhy*. "It could be worth nothing in two days."

Stephens feels that Trump's political success can be traced to the same personal branding that is behind his business success. He compares the "authentic" association of the Trump brand with the rise of the craft beer industry: the desire by consumers and voters alike to cut through the generics.

While Stephens sees robust strength in Trump's personal brand, he sees a dangerous risk for it as the election and associated negative press continues.

"Branding is much more fragile when it comes to individuals," states Stephens. "There's a human being in the middle of it, and that human being is as volatile as anything."

Stephens highlights the way Trump's increased personal and business profile has the potential to magnify any missteps he may make. Trump has made strong inroads based on his aggressiveness, but "even that could go too far."

O. C. Ferrell, the distinguished chair of Business Ethics at Belmont University and co-author of *Principles of Marketing*, agrees that Trump's political actions have solidified his brand, but he disagrees with the notion that this is a misstep.

"I think he's too smart to do these kinds of things accidentally. He's getting millions and millions of dollars in terms of publicity." And, Ferrell points out, people usually forget negative associations with a brand over time, leaving just the success in people's memories.

Trump's bad publicity has already had business ramifications in the short run. The mogul has lost endorsement from many sources over some of his racially charged comments. But even with NBC dropping Trump from *The Apprentice* and Univision ending its partnership with Trump's Miss Universe pageant, Ferrell nevertheless sees Trump as extremely business-savvy.

"The people that dropped him—he was probably ready to end those [relationships]," Ferrell told *WhoWhatWhy*. So what is a big complaint?

"What he's doing will probably increase his brand identity," contends the marketing professor. "Something there in the business captures part of the voting population. He comes across as authentic." Because the voters think, "Everyone's fed up with politicians trying to appeal to everyone."

But things may not go smooth with Trump and his controversy. Jonah Berger, a teacher in Duke's Fuqua School of Business, has shown that controversy is a double-edged sword for brands. As he points out, "While a little garners attention, too much can hurt," and "Mr. Trump's juicy sound bites—which successfully drew attention away from his opponents and made him the focal point for the race early on—are now perilously close to branding him a zealot out of step with American values."

Indeed, Mr. Berger's research indicates that when you are lesser-known to the public, even some negative publicity can be a good thing, because it raises the level of your overall brand awareness. Trump entered the race as a celebrity, but he was not established as a politician and his policy views and numbers are still relatively unknown, so early controversy may well have been helpful. But as you become more famous, negative publicity begins to stick, and hurts. So is the case with Donald Trump now.

Mel Carson, founder of *Delightful Communications*, a personal branding firm, points out that building the brand's visibility is unhelpful to Trump if it becomes too fraught with negative associations. A bigger brand means more people recognizing what it represents.

"Trump has overstepped the line in his eagerness to get some press over the other nominees," he told *WhoWhatWhy*. While Trump's rhetoric is winning him success with a certain subset of the American populace in this political campaign, observes Carson, his antics will likely hurt him in the business world.

"He's gonna have put a lot more notoriety around himself and what he's said," Carson says. "There are some people in this country with extreme views who are going to believe him. But people with influence in the business world and brands are not going to."

Carson thinks that Trump's reputation may be hard hit by foreign clients.

"Any press about what he's saying around the world will be centered on the negativity. If people are talking about it in the UK, I can guarantee that it has had a negative effect on America. 'Look at these crazy Americans!'"

Still, Carson suspects that even with these hits to his business brand, Trump's properties may not suffer, since real estate remains a tangible business, rooted in reliable properties and hands.

"I don't think he's going to lose anything, but he's not going to gain from it. The negativity of his personal brand has been solidified in many people's views."

To Kevin Lane Keller, E. B. Osborn Professor of Marketing at the Tuck School of Business at Dartmouth College and author of *Strategic Brand Management: Building, Measuring, and Managing Brand Equity*, Trump's monopoly of headlines means that any missteps he makes will be nearly impossible to live down.

"If for whatever reason he becomes tainted, he sort of gets tagged, no matter what happens in the future," Keller told *WhoWhatWhy*. He suggests that the Internet has changed how long negative press lasts. In any Internet search for a person involved in a scandal, previous news stories stick around. "There's so much more media in various forms. It's kinda hard to shake."

More people are getting entertaining news on Trump because of broader media access that Trump has been applying his marketing strategies for. Ten years ago, less than 18 percent of the world's population had access to the Internet. Last year, roughly 3 billion people, approximately 43 percent of world population, were online. This is a phenomenal growth, and the pace of change continues help Trump attract more people to him than through the TV medium.

Keller thinks the real danger comes when business negotiations begin to be influenced by the version of Trump seen in the campaign. "People have to feel at least some level of comfort with the brand to get involved with the property," he says.

"I don't know why people would ever trust him with anything." Keller continued.

But Trump is best known for increasing the value of his fortune through real estate deals and development. The Trump Organization currently has stakes in casinos, golf courses, residential housing, hotels, and resorts around the globe. He's made money by making these deals, selling properties for a tidy profit, and by promoting the Trump brand itself. Donald Trump's time spent on *The Apprentice* and in other celebrity guest appearances only further enhanced the public recognition and appeal of his brand.

Donald Trump generally prefers to invest in real estate and construction—and few would argue that he doesn't know what he is doing. But real estate, over the long term, may not be as strong an investment as some people and investors think.

Whether he wins or does not win the US Presidency, there are some factors going to hurt his empire:

1. If the lenders feel fed-up, investors in Trump Organization begin to sell their shares or stakes.
2. He fails to regain the reign of Taj Mahal, the center of his business and branding.

3. Financial revenge: he stepped on so many million people's feet, they won't spare him easily. If they can, they will get at him.
4. Divorce of the third marriage. His divorce of the second marriage cost him almost a half of his fortune.
5. Fall and cancellation in his new business licensing and in his unique branding.
6. The fall of the worth of the existing branding: good will.
7. Step-mother like behavior from the Wall Street.

But as a businessman, Trump is a fighter. He bounced back successfully a couple times and he will do again, a general expectation from his long past.

Donald has created turbulence for his own empire, which can sustain a certain number of strikes. This dark monster is his own creation. He is his own architect, and he is the destroyer of his own empire, its Frankenstein. He has almost done so in the past. Now is different, because he has created more enemies everywhere on the globe. How far can he go and how much he can gain from the US political institutions' norms and traditions?

The moral downfall of his empire has already been made. Trump is solely responsible for it. This has made him either the most idiotic business person or the most successful, hurting, difficult-to-understand type business psycho-gem. But Donald's branding knows well how to survive a deadly American imperial war and the harsh reality of the business world. The missing point here, he is in a hot seat in the game of politics.

But Why Does Donald Do It?

Donald Trump is not only a famous and successful businessman, but also is a writer. He has published sixteen books online. He is a thinker, a designer and manipulator about his strategies and plans.

Donald Trump's generations-long business branding doesn't indicate stupidity, so it must be for a business purpose. Or are we still missing something?

Or is he overconfident that he will win the election? That may seem reasonable to him. Under Obama, America has been safe from foreign terrorist attacks, and he has reduced warfare. Many disconnected, unhappy people have been waiting for a focus for their hate and anger.

Or, maybe, he did not listen to anyone, none of his advisors. One of his advisers has sued him for two million dollars. Nevertheless, Trump enjoys taking risks, pushing the limits, and seems to thrive on excitement. Such people are hard to work with because they are reckless, downplay their mistakes, take ill-advised risks, and have no regrets, like bad robots. He likes to act on his own, and is reluctant to listen to feedback, especially negative feedback from others.

As said earlier, there is a widening gap between the White House's empty promises, mediocre economic performance and apprehensive foreign policy, and US constituents who have become indifferent to their government, political system or even to their country. Trump came to the stage with a bang and has woken them up. Things are working for him so far.

During the first debate, he said quite demeaning things about his presidential rivals. One example was when Trump told Carly Fiorina that he doesn't like her looks, and he also told fellow presidential candidate Jeb Bush that he has "low energy."

He also targeted other politicians, even those who were not running for president. He has previously taunted Senator John McCain for his capture in Vietnam.

While it may be confusing to some people why *The Apprentice* host does these things, it seems pretty clear as far as psychologists are concerned. "The Trump campaign has used a whole bunch of tricks from reality television to run his campaign and extend control over other people's campaigns," says Robert Thompson, founder of the Bleier Center for Television and Popular Culture at Syracuse University in New York.

Based on the opinions of several famous psychologists, this attitude of Trump toward others is one of the main symptoms of narcissistic personality disorder.

Howard Gardner, a developmental psychologist and Harvard professor, said in an interview with *Vanity Fair* that he considers Donald Trump to be "remarkably narcissistic."

Another psychologist, Ben Michaelis, described Trump as someone having "textbook narcissistic personality disorder."

Michaelis further explained that narcissism is a personality disorder that is similar to others in its "cluster," some of which include histrionic, borderline, and antisocial personality disorders.

These types of personality disorders make the person anti-social, aggressive, and incapable of feeling remorse even after "attacking" or "degrading" a person verbally or psychologically without any remorse and with a personal goal.

Every fascist is a narcissist. Narcissism is another important tenet of fascism, because crazy ideas must come from a crazy head without remorse and respect.

Or is this Trump's revenge on the Republican Party, who didn't allow him to run for presidential candidacy in 2012? It doesn't seem to be right the way Trump is attracting his voters and staying on top in the Republican Party band wagon.

It's a shame that a large number of US citizens love him and they won't go away from the US politics with their hateful comments, aggressive behavior and a fascist mind, even if Trump fails.

But nothing is the end of this win-win race. Trump's provocative, aggressive campaign shows good results, but anytime it may turn to be a political gaffe if it puts pressure on the Democrats to come out to the polling stations in a larger number.

That will be the demise of Donald Trump for now, but not of his passionate followers.

And accepting Donald Trump campaign lightly that he will be beaten in the Presidential campaign! If the Democratic Party of US does it then this will be a political quagmire. Assuming that the Trump candidacy, that of a comic and surprising character, will fail in the US Presidential election of November 2016, the fact of its happening may still be the most tragic mistake the US will ever make, and no one need to look any further than the publicly documented words and actions of the man himself to see just how true that is. And truth may not win in the mix of anti-intellectualism, hatred and Muslim-terrorist-ghost fear that prevails in the U.S. This means America's democracy is at stake.

There is no correct time to oppose violence, prejudice and hatred.

However, because of the drawn-out wars by Bush, economic struggles, exploding debt, rising unemployment, hyperinflation, and the severe decline in political culture led by Trump, it is easy to point to these signs and conclude that America is in an irreversible economic and political decline. But this ignores the nation's history of resilience—the brilliance of American spirit. Our expectation is that America's decline will be a myth, and hopeful that things will turn around, the right person will be elected as the US President, the world will sigh in relief and we will enjoy a unique brand of hegemonic US leadership in a brave new world.

This world needs you, good Americans.

The End

www.ingramcontent.com/pod-product-compliance
Lightning Source LLC
Chambersburg PA
CBHW071405280526
45787CB00001B/437